SHAMANIC WISDOMKEEPERS

SHAMANISM IN THE MODERN WORLD

TIMOTHY FREKE

SHAMANIC WISDOMKEEPERS

SHAMANISM IN THE MODERN WORLD

TIMOTHY FREKE

A GODSFIELD BOOK

Library of Congress Cataloging-in-Publication Data Available

10 9 8 7 6 5 4 3 2 1

Published in 1999 by Sterling Publishing Company, Inc.
387 Park Avenue South, New York, N.Y. 10016
© 1999 Godsfield Press
Text © 1999 Timothy Freke

Tim Freke asserts the moral right to be identified
as the author of this work.

Distributed in Canada by Sterling Publishing
c/o Canadian Manda Group, One Atlantic Avenue, Suite 105
Toronto, Ontario, Canada M6K 3E7
Distributed in Australia by Capricorn Link (Australia) Pty Ltd
P O. Box 6651, Baulkham Hills, Business Centre, NSW 2153, Australia

Printed and bound in Hong Kong

ISBN 0-8069-9913-6

Acknowledgements

I would like to express my heartfelt gratitude to all the remarkable men and women who
were generous enough with their wisdom to participate in this book, and to all the many people who
assisted in so many ways, including: my mother Ellen Freke for patiently typing up all the interviews,
Debbie Thorpe, Sandy Breakwell, Donna Wood, Sally Adams, Jane Alexander, and all those at
Godsfield Press and Bridgewater Books, my agent Susan Mears, my spiritual brother Peter Gandy
for his endless inspiration, my partner Deborah O'Shea for her love and support, Nicholas Wood editor
of the excellent Sacred Hoop magazine, Dominic Findlay, Mark Goodman, Hugh Newton, Nick Ryan,
Peter Terry, Diana Griffiths, Mike Bonser, Michelle Pilley, Shelagh Keleyhers, Stephen Schoff,
Kate Roddick, Sobonfu Somé, Bert Gunn, Jan Adamson, Annie Spence.

MITAKUYE OYASIN—WE ARE ALL RELATED

CONTENTS

Introduction   *page 6*

Jamie Sams
Cherokee and Seneca Traditions   *page 10*

Malidoma Patrice Somé
West African Dagara Tradition   *page 24*

Miguel A. Kavlin
Amazonian Tradition   *page 38*

Haleakala Hew Len, Ph.D.
Hawaiian Tradition   *page 52*

Lama Khemsar Rinpoche
Tibetan Yungdrung Bon Tradition   *page 64*

Andy Baggott
Celtic Tradition   *page 80*

Aiko Aiyana
Santo Daime Tradition   *page 92*

Martín Prechtel
Tzutujil Mayan Tradition   *page 104*

Ernesto Alvarado
Apache Tradition   *page 118*

Lorraine Mafi-Williams
Australian Aboriginal Tradition   *page 130*

Addresses   *page 142*

INTRODUCTION

Shamanism is the primal ground from which all spiritual traditions have emerged. It is the ancient religion of our ancestors, who took nature as their spiritual teacher. It has no sacred scriptures or dogmas. It is a living wisdom rediscovered by countless generations of nameless adventurers who have explored the hidden terrains of consciousness and glimpsed the vastness of reality.

Despite centuries of brutal colonialism in which Shamanism has been attacked as diabolical superstition, indigenous communities have kept the heart of their traditional wisdom beating. Today it is these perennial teachings that may save the modern world from asphyxiating itself with the toxic by-products of its own ignorance. For, as we rush headlong into the abyss of environmental catastrophe, Shamanism reminds us of the fragile beauty of the web of life; that creation is not a resource to be coerced into fulfilling our insatiable appetites, but a living wonder to be respected. It roots us in our common mother the Earth; reawakening an awareness of all living things as her extended family, not products in some factory farm. While contemporary society fragments, Shamanism refreshes ancient memories of harmonious human community and offers us hope.

The western world, dominated by scientific materialism and consumerism, has amassed extravagant wealth to conceal a spiritual vacuum. But the profound enigmas of existence have not gone away and ever greater numbers of people yearn for more meaning than the fleeting world of fashion and gimmicks can possibly provide. Shamanism answers this fundamental need. It teaches us to reach below the surface of modern superficialities and reconnect with something old and mysterious within the depths of our soul.

This book contains the insights of some remarkable pioneers who have taken up the challenge of making this archaic wisdom accessible to the modern world. It is not a book about shamans, but a book that allows shamans to speak for themselves.

I have not selected the contributors, but simply held a vision of the sort of book I wished to collate and the right people have emerged. The result is the extraordinary cross-section of shamanic experience presented in these interviews. As with all forms of spirituality, Shamanism is littered with charlatans and wanna-bes. But I feel honored to present in this book human beings of genuine integrity.

Some of these shamans are internationally famous teachers and authors. Some of them live more anonymous lives, committed to their own spiritual journey and helping others whenever they can. All of them offer us their personal perspectives on the many-sided nature of Shamanism. I have not attempted to edit these interviews into perfect prose, but have retained the idiosyncratic speech patterns of the speaker to allow the reader to share in something of the immediacy of conversing with these powerful personalities. This book does not outline a coherent overview of Shamanism. That may be impossible. What it does do is allow practicing shamans to share some of their thoughts in an informal and personal way.

I have not attempted to force these conversations down preordained avenues, but have given each shaman the opportunity to communicate freely about the particular aspects of Shamanism he or she feels to be important. Jamie Sams points us away from a superficial preoccupation with supernatural phenomena and toward the omnipresent magic of life. Malidoma Somé confronts us with the concrete reality of spirit beings. Miguel Kavlin reveals the vision-inducing power of ayahuasca, an Amazonian power plant. Haleakala Hew Len presents us with Ho'oponopono, an ancient Hawaiian technique of spiritual transformation. Lama Khemsar Rinpoche teaches us to have indiscriminate love for all beings, including the spirits. Andy Baggott offers healing through eating in harmony with nature. Aiko Aiyana shares her experiences as part of the congregation of the Santo Daime church, a synthesis of psychedelic Shamanism and Christianity.

Martín Prechtel returns us to an indigenous understanding of the shaman as a spokesman for the village in the spirit world. Ernesto Alvarado brings us back to the basic humanity of treating each other as family. Lorraine Mafi Williams explains that, according to the Aboriginal tradition, we are in a period of extraordinary change which will give birth to a "new world."

The life-journey of each of these shamans has encompassed both indigenous Shamanism and contemporary western culture. Lama Khemsar Rinpoche was born into a living shamanic tradition in Tibet and then thrust into the modern world after the occupation of his country by the Chinese. Andy Baggott, by contrast, is a westerner reconnecting to his indigenous Celtic tradition, which has been all but lost under the debris of history. Martín Prechtel was a practicing shaman and headman in a small Guatemalan village for fourteen years, before becoming a teacher in the Men's Movement in the US. Ernesto Alvarado is a practicing psychologist as well as an Apache medicine man. Many contributors are not only masters of traditional wisdom, but also hold prestigious degrees from western universities. Malidoma Somé, for example, was born in a remote African village where he underwent a powerful traditional shamanic initiation, but went on to study at the Sorbonne in Paris.

The experiences of these shamans form a bridge between the ancient and modern worlds, leading us back to forgotten wisdom. They are the whispering voices of the ancestors in the confused cacophony of the modern maelstrom. In this epoch of spiritual sleep, they are our wake-up call—rousing us from muted mundanity and urging us to become more alive. Their inspiring testimonies coax us out of the narrow confines of "normality" into an expansive communion with nature. The nature of the world we live in. The nature of our own essential being. The nature of the Great Mystery that is life.

Timothy Freke

JAMIE SAMS
CHEROKEE AND SENECA TRADITIONS

Jamie Sams is an internationally respected Native American teacher. She is the author of many bestselling books including *The Thirteen Clan Mothers* and *Dancing the Dream*, as well the cocreator of the innovative "Medicine Cards" and "Sacred Path Cards." She is half-blooded Cherokee on her father's side and half-blooded Seneca on her mother's, with a Mohawk great grandmother and a Choctaw great grandmother.

Jamie experienced other levels of reality from an early age, which attracted the attention of both her tribal elders and western researchers into parapsychology. Although she herself had no desire to be a shaman, Spirit had other ideas. Through a magical sequence of events she ended up studying with a number of extraordinary teachers who helped her to develop her natural shamanic abilities. These teachers were a Mexican shaman, Joaquin Muriel Espinosa, and two Kiowa grandmothers, Cisi Laughing Crow and Berta Broken Bow. When Jamie was 22, Cisi was about 120 years old and Berta 127! Both were born shortly after the Trail of Tears in the 1840s when their families, refusing to be confined to reservations, traveled south to find freedom in the Mexican mountains. Here they were able to keep their traditions alive—an ancient lineage of which Jamie is now a living representative.

Jamie is a dynamic and charismatic communicator, with a gift for presenting indigenous teachings in ways easily accessible to the modern world. Drawing on the riches of all the different tribal traditions that have touched her life she teaches an inspiring synthesis of Native American wisdom, which goes to the heart of the perennial spirituality of Shamanism. Her earthy and often ribald sense of humor cuts through spiritual pretensions to reveal the everyday magic of living in communion with the Great Mystery. For Jamie, each one of us can become a shaman in our own way, by discovering and nurturing our own particular gifts from Spirit. She teaches Native American Shamanism as a spiritual path which, if walked with sincerity, can help us live in natural harmony with all of life.

Oh keeper of ancient knowing,
Whisper your wisdom to me,
That I may remember,
Life's sacred mystery.

WISDOMKEEPER PRAYER
Jamie Sams

LISTENING TO WISDOMKEEPER JAMIE SAMS

"The goal of Shamanism is total and complete merging your spirit within the whole and finding your place within the whole. You are still a human spirit but you acknowledge that you have a meat body that is connected to the animals, nature, and every other part of the universe."

"I was moving objects with my mind when I was three years old and I became the lab rat. My family is a very educated family. Education was the most important thing for the past four generations of my family. My great grandmother was one of the first Native American women to graduate from

Time-lapse photograph of the bustle of Mexico City by night.

college in the United States in 1886. So we were connected to various universities and when this phenomena started happening the parapsychology departments in various universities started doing tests on me. I don't know how to explain the fact that I have always seen energy around objects.

"It was my grandfather who decided that I should be trained with the elders. I just wanted to fit into modern everyday society. At one time I was living in Hollywood, California, and I wanted more than anything else to sing.

"But Spirit said: 'No way!' When you're doing the wrong thing everything is an effort. Your body will suffer and your health will suffer—running up against a brick wall and splatting time and time again. It's always like that if you are not doing what is authentically right for you. It's a real hard lesson because you didn't get your heart's greatest joy and Spirit has another plan for you.

"I ended up training with three elders in Mexico for three and a half years. The only reason

12

Yucca trees in the Mexican desert
on the Baja California peninsula.

I stopped was that I fell through a roof and was paralyzed from the waist down. People said: 'She will never walk again'. But my teachers worked on me and I was walking in three months! One of my teachers was Joaquin Muriel Espinosa. He was truly an amazing person. One of the things he told me was that the person who has actually integrated with life can shape-shift. They have taken all of creation into themselves and can walk in the snow without leaving a footprint. I have seen my shape-shifter teacher Joaquin shift into the form of an owl right in front of my eyes. He used that ability to check up on people he had done healings with who lived a long, long way away. It came as naturally to him as breathing does to you or me."

Jamie's teachers helped her develop her awareness of more subtle forms of perception. One of their techniques was to require her to sit still and simply observe the world for up to eight hours without blinking! Such demanding trials taught her how to clearly perceive the spiritual "energies" which permeate creation and enter into a silent communion with nature.

"Shamanism is fairly misunderstood by the western world because they are looking for the physical reality of what a healer or holy person taps into when they are trying to access the spirit behind a physical object. Many of the indigenous tribes take people who are gifted and use power substances, in the way of ayahuasca, herbs, mushrooms, and various things, to strip away the third dimensional perception, so they see the patterns—which are basically lines of energy that come together in different ways. With those patterns there are sound connections. There can also be visuals. Like the face of an animal coming forward to the person and going into the person's body.

"My teachers, when they started me, would sit me on one of the busiest intersections in a big city in Mexico. And they would make me sit without blinking for about five minutes. And maybe in five minutes 150 people would walk by

Tarahumara tribeswoman near her cave home in Creel, Chihuahua State, Mexico.

and they'd say: 'How many people walked by that were wearing the color pink?' And that was the first lesson. And so you extend your perception peripherally with your eyes. You have to also perceive every single thing around you in a different way. They worked me up to sitting eight hours without moving, blinking, twitching. And then they upped the gradient. Like asking: 'How many

"It's not about 'me.' It's about 'we.'"

people walked by who had a disability?' And of course they knew the answers! 'How many people walked by who had a life-threatening disease and a hole in their dreaming body?' 'How many people walked by who were holding a death wish?' 'How many people walked by who were fulfilled and happy?' And on and on until I could take it all in. It was observing the obvious and then observing energy—the intangible and the physical together.

"When you blink, the optic nerve acts as a shutter mechanism in between the brain. The more you blink the more you are recreating the solidity in front of you. When the mind is clear and you're not blinking, then there is space for your body to perceive the other sensory perceptions that go beyond the five senses. There are 357 invisible threads that

The South American jaguar,
seen here in the Mexican rain forest,
is an endangered species.

go all the way around the body from the center of the navel, which is the dreaming body. These perceive and then take what they are perceiving and funnel it into the brain so you can see it. Blinking creates the thought processes going 'yak yak yak' in your head which stops you from perceiving other things which are not tangible but which are connected to all solid matter.

"It's a real different world out there when you can see the energy surrounding every living thing. You see that everything is interconnected. Everything is alive. And once you experience that wholeness no one can take it away from you. There is a new-found deep, deep respect for every living thing that allows you to walk gently on the earth and in harmony, and experience life with ease. Even if the most dramatic, chaotic experiences come and land on your doorstep you can still move through them, because you see them as opportunity instead of tragedy. This is part of understanding that life is an initiation."

As in other shamanic traditions, the Native American tradition teaches that we can learn much wisdom from our "relatives" the animals. Jamie is well known for making these ancient teachings accessible in a thoroughly modern way in her "Medicine Cards." These help people connect with the animal spirits which are particularly relevant to them in their spiritual evolution.

"One of the things that draws people to this path is that they can see nature all around them. Even if a person lives in the city, they have at some time in their life been in nature. And almost everyone loves the animals. I think that it's important that every human being understand that they can tap into the animals and to nature. And that it's another form of paying tribute to the God

in all things—the spark of life that the Creator put inside of every living thing. And once they can honor that sacredness they are able to see that same spark, what we call the Eternal Flame of Love, within themselves.

"In our tradition every human being has nine power animals that they are born with, and these animals represent nine different facets of their personality, and why they are here, as well as their gifts, talents, and abilities that they can share with the world. Some of these talents or traits can be very undeveloped. You are here for a reason, which is to learn these skills and develop these gifts and talents to the point that you can then share them with others and make a difference within the human condition for the better.

"My teachers taught me the animals through drum beats. They showed me the patterns of energy that were connected not only to the way the animals walked but to the energy that the animals carried. And they would do certain drum beats and ask: 'What animal came to you when you were listening to this?'

"Everything has a pattern. You have a pattern. I have a pattern. My grandfather taught me this when I was seven years old. He threw a rock into a pond and asked me what I saw. I said that I saw a splash in the water. And he said: 'Good, what else did you see?' And I said I saw circles.

Ladder up to cliff house, Bandelier National Monument, New Mexico.

A little circle and then a bigger circle until it came all the way out to the edge of the pond. He said: 'Good. What I want you to know is that you have to be very careful about the kind of splash you make in the world because your individual circle will touch another circle all the way out to the shore. So what kind of splash are you going to make? What is in your circle individually that you can share with others?'"

"Walk your talk.
Don't talk your walk."

The ineffable Power of Life which we call "God" is conceptualized in various ways by different spiritual traditions, but its essential nature is perhaps most eloquently expressed by the evocative Native American phrase the "Great Mystery." For Jamie, the goal of Shamanism is not to possess special magical abilities, but to transcend the self and commune with the Great Mystery. If we do this, then all of life becomes magical.

"Some people choose not to help others. They choose to develop their gifts so they can have material things. To be respected as: 'Gee! I'm the shaman. I'm the healer.' And the old ego stuff comes in here. Some people get stuck in not healing themselves. They get stuck in revenge so that

Copper Canyon, the awesome descent into
Batopilas Canyon above La Bufa, Mexico.

they feel they are in competition with everyone else. They use the same beautiful gifts, which could help people, to harm another person. That is very common, especially in indigenous communities.

"Many people get to the place where they say: 'I know my power animal' or 'I have these abilities'—but they never relinquish the human identity into the infinite identity of being a perfect part of Spirit within all of creation. I think that it's very important that people who are looking at Shamanism realize that being a shaman is not the goal. The goal is to access their place in the whole of creation. It's not to be a shaman. 'I am a shaman' —that statement creates separation.

"If a person is looking for a way to connect to what we call the Great Mystery—the continual evolving universe—and to tap into the 'Dream Weave' and the Spirit within all things, they have to begin by illuminating places they have sent their own spirit into expressing revenge or envy or any of the unbecoming attitudes and behavior patterns that further separation. So it always begins with the self. You may not be able to change society or save the planet, but you can correct your own behavior so that you walk in an impeccable manner with respect for all living things. And that is the goal.

"Life is magic. Sometimes people get stuck in what we call an enlightenment trap. In the phenomena. In 'Oh I can make this happen or that happen!' Well, where is that centered? In ego. The phenomena is just part of the process. It shows us that life is refunding us with signals and acknowledgements. If we use our spirit in a proper manner, then we are going to feel that everything is magic, and that miracles are possible, and that every single thing that we do in life can help the whole.

"There are a lot of dabblers these days —weekend warriors."

"If there is inner peace there is connectedness. When it's still and quiet inside we call it 'Tiyoweh' which means the 'Stillness.' If you cannot be thinking of anything, you're in present time. Then you become a part of the harmony in nature and nature's creatures will acknowledge you without fear. You can literally stop the world and an animal will walk up within two or three feet of you and look you straight in the eye, and not be afraid. And you will see that you can get rid of all the separation and be in communion."

The brilliantly colored flowers
of the aloe vera plant.

"Be here now. Accept the fact that nature, this universe, the Creator, and the Earth Mother are all supporting your spirit's evolution. Sit with your back against a tree—anywhere. It can even be a city park. Just observe everything around you without blinking. Do it first for a short period of time and work up to an hour. My teachers made me stay in stillness for eight hours. If you can sit out in nature without blinking you will see things—like a light around trees. You will start being able to perceive the energy in animals."

MALIDOMA PATRICE SOMÉ
WEST AFRICAN DAGARA TRADITION

Malidoma Patrice Somé is a truly remarkable man who has lived an extraordinary life. Born in a small traditional village of the Dagara people in West Africa, he was kidnaped by French Jesuit missionaries at the age of four and spent the next fifteen years in a Catholic boarding school. Here he was indoctrinated into the ways of the white man until, at the age of twenty, he escaped and returned to his people. In order to reintegrate himself into his own culture he risked his life to undergo a month-long shamanic initiation—a demanding ordeal during which some other young initiates died. At the age of twenty-two the tribal elders asked him to return to the white man's world to understand it more fully and to share with us what he had learned about the Dagara spiritual tradition. He began by studying at a local university, before receiving a scholarship to study at the Sorbonne and then Brandeis University. He now holds three master's degrees and two doctorates.

The Dagara believe that every individual comes into this life with a special destiny, and that often a person's "life project" is inscribed in their name. The Dagara name "Malidoma" means "Be friends with the stranger/enemy." Malidoma's role has been to do just this. He brings the shamanic wisdom of the Dagara as a gift to the white man. To the logical western mind his fantastical stories of strange otherworldly events may strain credibility, but to meet Malidoma is to be confronted with a man of exceptional integrity. An emissary who humbly offers his experiences and insights as a part of Africa's contribution to the communal human endeavor of understanding the profound mysteries of existence.

Malidoma has broken the traditional secrecy surrounding African shamanic practices to relate the strange story of his childhood and initiation in his wonderful autobiography *Of Water and the Spirit*. This astonishing book is a unique insight into a world in which spirits are commonplace and magic is part of daily life. Although writing his book was a painful process undertaken with deep misgivings, he regards it as essential that the voice of Africa is heard at last and its wisdom understood, before it is lost for ever.

KA TI SANKUN KORO BA KA A TI ZIE,
KA TI TUON GNERE,
TI BAON A TI GNOVURU SOR NA GNA LE NA.

May our ancestors breathe blessing onto
us for our eyes to open,
and our life purpose to become clear.

DAGARA PRAYER

Ashanti chief's witch doctor at the Akwasidae Kesee Festival, Kumasi, Ghana.

"I've taken a huge, huge risk in exposing myself in the way that I did in my book. So many times I found myself in tears, but my hand could not stop writing."

"There is a wisdom in the African continent that has not been crystallized into coherent western language in order to participate in the concert of cultural philosophy that is going on. There are certain concepts and certain realities that I don't even have a word for. And they're some of the most exciting parts.

"The novelist Joseph Conrad was right in calling Africa the dark continent because even when you're in it and you watch the people, there's still a mystery around what it is that Africans really believe in. Because when you look at it from the outside it has the look of superstition. When translated literally, it just doesn't echo. It doesn't make sense. And this is because a lot of African spirituality is surrounded by silence and hiddenness. As if there is a fear that disclosure will disempower the material immediately. And so there is a collective approach to shamanic power as a thing that is kept alive under the mantle of silence. And they do that very well.

"This is the reason why among some of my worst critics are Africans who think I've disempowered African Shamanism by exposing it in this manner. And to some degree they're right. But we are moving into an extremely accelerated time that requires world cultures to come together to create a certain unity in this world. In that context they're not right. They are not keeping up with the reality that is happening. In this kind of situation, if Africa doesn't contribute there will be a huge missing link somewhere. And it's not right to keep something surrounded by secrecy indefinitely, because the inevitable changes that are coming may change that thing into the irrecoverable dust of silence."

For the Dagara, Shamanism is not a part of life, but provides an understanding that embraces all of life. Shamanism is more than beliefs and rituals. It is an experiential investigation of the invisible spirit world which gives rise to the tangible world of the senses.

"In Africa, particularly among the people of my tribe, life is Shamanism. Every single event in life is viewed within a spiritual context. The cycle of life includes two aspects. One is palpable, tangible. The other one is nonpalpable, nontangible. Both are so interdependent that, more often than not, the experience of the visible part of life is triggered by the nonvisible. Shamanism is a response to the challenge of understanding the language of the invisible world as it transpires into the visible world. Nature is kept the way it is from fear of losing very significant data by messing with it.

"The exciting part of life in the village is right in that invisible area of existence, because there is still so much there to be learned. Basically, from the creation story to the manner in which social interactions are conducted, the source of the inspiration has not come from experience of this world, but from understanding the other world."

Malidoma teaches that African Shamanism places great importance on emotion. Although seemingly very otherworldly, it is actually completely focused on improving the quality of life in the here and now of this world.

Villagers smoking and preserving fish on the coast of Ghana.

"Shamanism is really driven by knowing of the existence of other intelligences."

"African spirituality is the missing link in the coming together of cultural wisdom that is going on, because it takes a great deal of the emotional being into account. If there is one thing that is quite irreplaceable in a human being, it's the capacity to emote. To carry emotion. To be able to feel. This is an extremely useful tool that needs to be explored in every direction possible. In the modern world there is a tendency to take little interest in the emotional self. The introduction of that makes a lot of difference, because all of a sudden the human being expands and becomes almost like a genius ready to do all kind of things. As if he's been hit by some kind of shock that opens the eyes into a new kind of usefulness.

"Shamanic processes in Africa are so life-orientated that basically they're not interested in escaping the karmic grip of the moment. They are interested in making the moment feel like paradise. They are interested in enjoying the present and the core of that interest is a desire to stretch life in this plane. And this is why shamanic processes are more worldly than otherworldly. So, when someone goes to the other world he's looking for recipes to bring back into this world in order to make it more pleasurable here.

"You go to the village and basically, by the kind of standards you live by, you realize these people are miserable. But when you get closer you realize they have the most magical things in the world. And then you start saying: 'Hey, maybe this is why they're not interested in the kind of pursuits that occupies our day-to-day life in the West.' Because the amount of joy they are able to wield with close to nothing is just unbelievable. I wouldn't have known it if I didn't have a little distance from it. So I could look down upon it and realize that this capacity comes from a nonmaterial perception of Life which uses Spirit as an exciting tool to enjoy the present."

Shamanism is not a form of spirituality based on moral codes of right and wrong behavior, but is about achieving a direct communication with other intelligences living in other dimensions. In Malidoma's tradition, the most important of these are the Kontombili—small spirit beings who regularly appear to guide and teach the Dagara.

"What I like about African spirituality is that it's not operating with the expectation of being included into the divine realm through good actions or some kind of good behavior. It is focused on developing a sort of diplomatic relationship with other intelligences that it knows

Native straw granaries in Burkina Faso.

"A shamanic object creates a certain weather around it.
I say 'weather' because I don't know what other term to use.
There's a vibration that, as you get closer, starts to affect
you and the body goes into hypervibration."

exist. Everyone knows they are there, except that some are more scared about them than others. I'm not scared because it's part of my family tradition.

"Right now in my family there is someone who's in charge of a relationship with the Kontombili. She can call and they can come over and we can talk. If I want to know something I just have to pick up the phone and call my sister and tell her what problem I'm going through and she'll pass it on to them. And they will show up here, check it all up, and go back there to have a ritual dance that will change the course of things here. Now how did that happen? I don't know. I just know that as long as it works for me I'm content.

"It is not subjective or far-fetched when people of my tribe talk about other beings, because they exist just like you and I exist. At one point I thought that maybe there was a trick somewhere which I am able to participate in because I am of the tribe. But I brought people from the West to go there and tell me whether I'm going nuts or something. And, lo and behold, they are able to see that

little being coming out of a rock telling them about things that are going on in their lives that, by western standards, they have no way of knowing—the kinda things that are considered secret or personal.

"These beings or these people are usually about a foot and a half tall—looking like you and I. A little red with hair. They have their racial features I would say. And they have told us that their life expectancy is at least five or six times that of us. The longest living one comes close to a thousand years. They don't just exist in Africa. They are everywhere. They are different, just the same as in each part of this world there are different types of people. But in terms of intelligent awareness and advancement they're the same. They participate in the same kind of consciousness—whatever it is."

Western psychologists and anthropologists often categorize shamanic experiences such as encountering a Kontombili as a form of psychological projection. Traditional cultures lack the conceptual vocabulary to understand shamanic events in these ways, so an experience is taken on face value. The language of

the Dagara does not even have the concept "fiction."
However, Malidoma cautions against a reductionist
approach which dismisses the Kontombili as a sort of
subjective illusion. In his own experience, and in that
of the westerners he has taken to his home in Africa,
these spirit beings are very real.

"My experience of Shamanism has been of the intense excitement involved. To the point where all my senses, including some that I don't know where they come from, are engaged. And it is because of that engagement that no one can convince me that this thing is not for real. It is a different type of experience to when I am seeing someone on a chair or something. It's a bigger type of experience that means you are included in it, but there is a larger version of yourself.

"Modern culture has an extremely rich language that can describe almost every aspect of a thing. Hence the creation of the idea of a psychological projection, the imaginative intuition, and this and that. The problem with shamanic culture is that what you perceive is what it is. There's a certain kind of immediacy that barely submits itself to any kind of dissection or analysis. But given this fact, for me witnessing and being translator to a westerner who was able to hold the hand of a being from the other world for about five minutes, in the course of which communication was imparted, helped me to realize that the

African shaman at
Niofouin, Ivory Coast.

*Peul native woman in traditional
dress, Burkina Faso.*

concreteness is not only limited to myself. It's not an exclusive thing, but it's a human thing. Therefore you'd be rather a reductionist to look upon these beings as a psychological projection. They're so concrete that where it leads my imagination to is not far from the western idea of extraterrestrials. Except that they don't show up on a flying saucer. They just are and they just occur.

"You see, every time I go home I have to have liquor. Why? Because when the Kontombili show up in the house they will drink liquor. Yes. The liquor disappears. I would have a bottle of vodka and put it in the shrine. The level was on top, but by morning it's down here. And I go out for a visit somewhere and when I come back the bottle is empty. Now to the western mind you can investigate everyone in the house to make sure that somebody is not drinking that liquor. But really, it is not the case.

"You see, I go to the cave in order to say hello to them. I put the bottle in the cave, then it just floats off and disappears. Later on the empty bottle is brought back and put down. It's just that I don't

"For some reason the Kontombili utilize the exits that are high up in the world to pump out from. As if these places are like antennae pointed to their world that they can use to transport themselves into this world. If Africa has to contribute something, it's going to be in helping to identify the parts of the world which constitute doorways to these beings."

see who is doing that. Now, at best they are doing that. In the worst case, it's still a very interesting phenomena. I tell you, whatever it is, it is fascinating to watch. And if Shamanism allows someone to be watching an object from this world defy gravity, I'd like to see and watch that. It's fascinating."

The Kontombili appear to be divine, but they are simply wiser beings who are themselves still spiritually evolving. They seem to have remarkable shamanic powers, but actually they are just in touch with deeper levels of reality which are open to all of us.

"Spirits are different layers of intelligence and powers, so overwhelming to us that we are right in giving them divine status because they are so far advanced. Closer to a cosmic state of reality. So it is normal for a human consciousness to aspire to higher layers of consciousness and view these beings who have already reached these levels as divine.

"But for them there is nothing shamanic about what they are doing. It's just that here is another species struggling to become better, who believe in and trust the existence of realities far beyond the one that the immediate eye can catch. They feel themselves allowed to impart bits of wisdom that become then utilized as cultural practices

African women carrying bowls of produce, Choggu Yapalsi, Ghana.

African women in traditional dress cooking out of doors, Choggu Yapalsi, Ghana.

or spiritual practices. It is because of their other-worldliness that we tend to have a religious attitude to them. But they themselves don't feel that way.

"To the question whether they are gods, the Kontombili say they are not. As to whether they are close to God, they say: 'No, God is still further away.' The only thing they will admit is that they are better than you and I, and that they will live longer. When you talk to the Kontombili to find out what the problem is, what's going on, what needs to be done, they say: 'It will work out if God wants it.'"

The Kontombili can appear anywhere at any time to those with the necessary clarity of consciousness to perceive them. They continue to play an important role in Malidoma's life, despite the fact that he now lives and works primarily in the US. Part of his mission is to introduce westerners to the idea that these spirit beings truly exist and it is possible for anyone who is open to the experience to communicate with them.

"They can show up anywhere. Whether you perceive them would depend on your state of mind. Put it this way, if you are agitated the chances are you will only hear them, but you won't see them. But if you have what I may call the quiet of a meditative posture, then all of a sudden you'd see a light. It's like a curtain gets moved and you

Healthy corn crop, Choggu Yapalsi, Ghana.

see the being. But at that moment it is impossible to both develop a critical attitude and yet keep locking on to them. You can only do one at a time. You start wondering: `What the hell is that?' And all of a sudden the curtain closes. Then you go back into a certain meditative posture, like cleaning up thoughts from your head, and all of a sudden the curtain opens again.

"The Kontombili say that the human problem is that its consciousness is too susceptible to distraction. Distraction has become a very big industry in the modern world. Instead, what they want is silence. Be quiet for a while and notice things going on. This is the reason why at the core of shamanic practice is a lot of time spent alone. It looks like alone, but in fact is not quite alone because there are all kinds of realities going on that you are examining.

"A shaman is somebody who is willing to engage the forces of the universe. At a very spiritual level, of course, we don't exist, nothing exists and nothing is real. It is an important thing to hold the notion of nonexistence on the one hand, because when you feel you are being trapped it is good to know you don't exist! Then you can't be trapped. It's ultimate freedom! But we don't live in nonexistence all the time. We do live in the created world. And it is beautiful to engage its manifold possibilities in creative and healing play. So I have no desire to just do without the created world. There are so many colors and smells and beings that you can work with that are wonderfully real.

"So a shaman is a person who has the capacity, the inclination, and the desire to engage the forces of the universe and can do so in a way that results in a beneficial end for himself, for people he is helping and for life in general. There are many different forces that can be used for each different purpose. Everywhere in the world has the sun and the moon in the sky, the earth beneath us, and the four directions all around us. So these are the main forces that shamans all over the world work with. But then there are other things, like beings from different planets, the stars, spiritual guides from many dimensions, the ancestors, as well as the spirits specific to places—brooks, waterfalls, mountain tops, ravines, etc.—and spirits of plants, animals, or stones. The only way that people from the western type of upbringing can appreciate the idea of spirits or gods is to experience them by feeling or seeing them. It is the only way. No explanation will do."

Miguel works with the Amazonian power plant ayahuasca which helps the shaman by opening up the subconscious mind. Taking this natural psychedelic

A Quiche Maya Native from Santa Catarina Palopo, Guatemala, in typically colorful dress.

is not about having a "good time," but about exploring inner space. It is not just a plant. It is sacred "medicine" which can reveal itself as a powerful spirit guide.

"I very much like to work with power plants. Power plants really take people beyond the place where they have control of their experience. They force the doors of the unconscious open, so people are really forced to face things that they would not allow themselves to face under normal circumstances. So that's one way to begin to find out what is real and what is not.

"Ayahuasca is not just a chemical reaction about which you can say: 'Well, it's good or it's bad. It works or it doesn't work.' It's got a spirit. Sometimes it reveals itself. Sometimes it doesn't. Sometimes it reveals itself to one person but not to another. This doesn't mean that the one person is any better than the other, because next time it could be the other way around. It has a logic completely of its own.

"When I say it reveals itself I mean it is bestowing you with its power and energy to enable

Crowded cloud rain forest in the eastern Andes of Bolivia.

you to go on the journey. And that can be different every time. It has two sides at least. It's difficult to describe. It's like the side of life and the side of death. And death is about purification. So most people are taken through an intense time of vomiting and discomfort. Dealing with their demons, and skeletons, and traumas, and all the things we have stored in our bodies since birth or even before. All the shit that we have to work through. The side of life is when you are lucky enough to be given a gift or a vision. Like one I had in a ceremony when I saw this sort of flower that turned itself into a geometrical pattern and opened up to me as my third eye. I knew it was a gift, so the next day I went looking for it. I knew it was a plant in the jungle. And I found it and made tea with it. Then I drank the tea."

"Life is really miraculous. Everything is alive and you can communicate with absolutely everything."

Miguel teaches that to take ayahuasca is to be purged and purified. It reaches deep inside and removes the layers of debris which obscure the soul, opening up the possibility of accessing psychic gifts we never knew we had.

Quiche Maya Natives selling flowers at Chichicastenango market in the Guatemalan highlands.

"The medicine will help you purify. You don't have to wait to be purified before taking the medicine, because then you wouldn't need the medicine. The ayahuasca goes into the body and starts to clean the body and the energies. Not just the physical body, but also the emotional body, the mental body, the spiritual body. And it starts to clean out. Whenever there is trauma in our lives a whole part of us goes dead—goes into our subconscious. We don't have access to it. So when you go and purify yourself, you begin to align yourself so that the energy can flow through. Then you are able to navigate, to focus, to have better concentration, to journey out of your body, to go places, to see things. These gifts are already inside but they are not accessible to us.

"I always get a kick when someone takes the medicine for the first time because I remember my own first time. It was so overwhelming to first open the doors of the subconscious and all the skeletons came pouring out! There was an outpouring of emotions and feelings and images. And I saw the good, the bad and the ugly. And more or less where I was coming from and where I was wanting to get to. So eventually you become more empty, as there are less things to come out. So you have more space to hold more of the universe within."

Living as we do in a culture paranoid about the use of drugs, shamanic power plants are sometimes dismissed as a dangerous and superficial form of spirituality. But Miguel rejects this entirely. Shamanic traditions have used ayahuasca and other sacred plants to engender profound mystical experiences for millennia. It is an ancient and completely natural form of spirituality.

"A lot of people might think that plants only let you work with limited or lower realms, but I don't think that's true. Some shamans work with very fine, sublime, lofty—or however you want to describe the highest realms. As with all practices, so with shamans, people work at all levels. There are cultural differences. Some describe themselves as working with divine energies and evoke Jesus and Mary. Some might say that others just work with spirits of the plants, as if that were somehow a lower rung of the profession. I'm not convinced of that. I have experienced plants as gateways to whole universes, and natives definitely held some plants to be vehicles of communication with the

"I've been asked if it is better to do the ceremonies in the jungle or in the cities, but wherever the miracles are going to happen they will."

Bright scarlet flowers amid the greenery of the Yungas highlands, Bolivia.

most sacred, as in the plants that make up the ayahuasca brew, or a kind of palm tree they believe connects them with the Milky Way and eventually to the Pleiades.

"I believe that the plants are sacraments. There are people that discount the material world and say all you can do is pray to God. Well, praying to God is a great thing. But God created the world. And not for nothing. So there is nothing wrong in us using what is in the created world to gain access. And some of the things that were created are special sacraments. The tribal people of the Amazon will tell you that ayahuasca was given to them by the gods in order to help them reconnect with mythical time and space—their divine origins. To me the bottom line is: 'Can you be beneficent and can you be effective?' If you can be these two things, then all the power to you!"

Much ancient shamanic wisdom has already been lost due to the westernization of indigenous communities. But Miguel teaches that even lost traditions remain alive and search out those to whom they can impart their wisdom. The spirits are waiting there for those courageous enough to contact them. But Shamanism can be dangerous. To those wishing to experiment with ayahuasca, Miguel recommends working with an experienced guide.

"Lots of things have been lost in many traditions. Knowledge that has been accumulated for a millennium. Sacred formulas and practices. Shrines that have not been fed every year as they

Stars seen against the night sky of Los Padres National Forest, Southern California.

"I try to honor the forces of the universe that they might find me a suitable helper to them, so we can heal one another and help all of life."

would have been before and so on. But I am an optimist and I do believe that even traditions that have a broken lineage of working with people, that tradition is seeking people to work with. So the right person with the right intent at the right time might reconnect with those forces and reenliven the tradition, although probably in quite a different way. So help is out there. But there is also danger out there. That is one of the reasons I don't want to just recommend that people take medicine.

"I started on my path on my own. It was fortunate that things went well, although I did have one particularly scary experience. You are opening up a Pandora's box. It is not for everybody and you've got to be ready to deal with whatever comes out. I would encourage undertaking this way with guidance. Although there really are people out there that could do it on their own. If they are strong enough. If they are courageous enough and lucky enough. I was lucky enough. But then I was very glad that I found the right

*Native dwellings on the high, arid upland plateau,
or altiplano, of Bolivia.*

context to give me the tools to help me along. But of course I can't sing victory. Anything can happen any day. One is never victorious until the last word is said. But it is important to acquire the tools to be able to navigate.

"The tools, in this particular case, are knowing how to work with energies. To know that purification is a very important part and that one is only as vulnerable as the transgressions you have committed. So if you are out there being really nasty and then take medicine—well anything can happen! Then some of the tools in Shamanism are the songs. And the tobacco which we use to clean other people, to suck out problems from people, to send out blessings and to send out defenses. Also the musical instruments. They are used to guide people on their journeys and to weave the energies of all the group. But the ultimate tools are inside. The wisdom, the ability to navigate, purification, and whatever resources one has—psychic, physical, emotional.

"In the West the context in which people can help you to have ayahuasca safely is not accessible or available. So a lot of people are having to go about it in the wrong way. But prayer in itself can be a great protection. If you do an offering and a prayer to each of the four directions, to Mother Earth, to the sky and to the Great Spirit, you are building up a good protection for yourself and that is very helpful."

Shamanism is about the intent with which something is done. Whether it be enduring the days and nights of fasting and dancing in the Sundance ritual or simply making a humble offering, what matters is our intention to give something back in gratitude for all that has been given to us.

"If you are doing a Sundance and you are not eating or drinking water for four days, and you

Andean women in the colorful woven dress and characteristic bowler hats of Bolivia.

"I hope to be of evermore service.
To be evermore guided to live the right way so I can be
empowered to help others. I hope to walk in grace. I've made
mistakes along my path which I have had to pay for.
Some people think that taking medicine is a shortcut to karma,
but doing all this work is not divorced from your daily life
and how you go about it. You have to live right as well.
So it's finding that line. And the more you walk,
the more impeccable you have to be."

are doing your best with intent to focus, you run out of fuel to lie to yourself and amazing things can happen. Or even just go out to your back area and pray and offer something and ask for help to come to you—and it can start to happen.

"This thing of offerings—I have run into it all over the world in different cultures. I think our culture is too biased in terms of construction, accumulation, life. And it doesn't give death its due. And death is the powers of destruction. It's fall and winter, which we need before we can have a spring. And it's the cycle of really giving and not just taking. It's like an exchange. We have to dislodge ourselves from our economy of accumulation, of taking and raping and pillaging, to an economy of giving and offering and being generous—a sort of sacrifice.

"We talk about this sort of sacrifice in the Bolivian Andes as 'payment.' You can talk about it in commercial terms if you want. It's pay-back. There used to be a festival after the harvest where you would give the first fruits of your harvest to the spirits as gratefulness. It rather depends on what your intent is. If you fill up a pipe with tobacco while you're thinking about steaks, this might not work. Whereas just a pile of earth with the right intent might work better. It really has to do with thankfulness and gratefulness and offering. That is like the Sundance. You are putting all your effort into the dance and you are suffering. This is your sacrifice. Some other cultures might sacrifice an animal. There are different ways to go about it."

Typical vegetation at Quinua Salar d'Oyrni, Bolivia.

The strange world of the shaman can seem a long way away from ordinary life in the modern West, yet Miguel sees our failure to honor our Mother Earth and our ancestral wisdom as the cause of much of our present social confusion and chaos. Given the will, it is still possible to reconnect to the shaman's world and refind the magic and mystery of life.

"They say that whatever you do unto others you do unto yourself. So, whenever you stop honoring the earth you are dishonoring yourself. Whenever you cut off your ties with your ancestors you are dishonoring yourself. You are disembowelling yourself. And this is why so many of us in the West are completely at a loss and looking for answers—including myself. We have forgotten a lot of things. So families get broken down. People don't relate to one another in harmonious ways any longer. We fight. The elderly get pushed into nursing homes. We rape and pillage the earth. So what can be done about it?

"I think we have to work from wherever we are and seek with the best possible intent to re-establish whatever connections we can; to know that we can feel the earth always underneath our feet and the sky above us. And that there are all kinds of beings around us. And if we believe that it is possible to establish relations with them by opening ourselves to them they will also give of themselves to us. We can start cultivating this in our lives, through prayers, through just the intent. You know you can get a transcendental message full of meaning coming toward you from the reflection of a neon sign on a puddle on the asphalt. If you believe that there is a purpose in life and you are willing to be touched by it, and you are paying attention, then you can find it everywhere."

Giant cacti are a feature of the landscape between Uyuni and Potosi in Bolivia.

HALEAKALA HEW LEN, PH.D.
HAWAIIAN TRADITION

A Hawaiian shaman is called a kahuna which means "keeper-of-secrets." In the old days there were kahunas who kept the sacred wisdom of everything from seed sowing to canoe building; as well as, of course, healing and spiritual illumination. Hawaii is now dominated by Christianity, but the traditions of the kahunas have survived underground. Those who still practice the old ways are usually very secretive about what they do. Not only because they mistrust nonindigenous people, but because they simply don't believe that we have the consciousness to really understand their teachings.

"The Foundation of I," however, is finally making the sacred principles of the kahunas accessible to the modern world. Haleakala Hew Len is the president of this organisation which was created to communicate these teachings. He has a distinguished presence, offset by the baseball cap that he habitually wears to remind himself "not to be an intellectual," and oozes wisdom and humility. He has worked with thousands of people over the years, including groups at the United Nations, UNESCO, and other international organizations; as well as with the disabled and the criminally insane and their families. In all of this work, he attributes his remarkable success to ancient Hawaiian shamanic practices.

Haleakala teaches that the magic of the kahunas stems from a profound understanding that everything is created by thoughts. Through having "errors" in our thoughts we misperceive reality, limiting both ourselves and others.

I am the "I"
I come forth from the void into light.
I am the breath that nurtures life.
I am that emptiness, that hollowness.
Beyond all consciousness.
The I, the Id, the All.
I draw my bow of rainbows across the waters,
The continuum of minds with matters.
I am the incoming and outgoing of breath.
The invisible untouchable breeze.
The undefinable atom of creation.
I am the "I."

<small>HAWAIIAN PRAYER</small>

LISTENING TO WISDOMKEEPER HALEAKALA HEW LEN

"When I was a very little kid I could see these things sitting on my crib. Floating through the air. They would talk to me. The flower would talk to me. The sky would talk to me. The ocean would talk to me. I had a grandma and we would go to the ocean and she would chant in Hawaiian. And the fish would come by the thousands out of nowhere and roll up on the beach. She would take the first one and give it back to the Light. And then she would take what she needed. The Hawaiians never had netting or hooks. They fished with their minds. That's not remarkable. It's something you can do. Really. It begins with thought.

"In the old ways of the Hawaiians there were different levels of kahuna. Different levels of what you folks would call 'shamans,' but there is no such word in Hawaiian. Now—I'm looking at this cup of coffee. The first level of kahuna could actually take that. Locate it with his mind. Crack that and take it down into shards. The next level of kahuna could look at that and be powerful enough to take it down into sand. And then there was another level who could actually take it down into just pure powder.

The scenic Akala Falls on Hawaii, surrounded by lush vegetation.

"It's an inside job. If you want to be successful, it's an inside job. Work on yourself."

"But there was an ultimate kahuna who could make this thing disappear. Just with his mind. This is what I'm talking about—the way I'm going to make that cup disappear. Since that cup is a perception of my thought, when my thought goes that cup will go. It'll go.

"If you are carrying an 'error' in your thoughts, you will perceive the world in a way that is not so. If I look at you and see you as this or that

A Hawaiian man, wearing a traditional necklace of shells, blows a conch horn.

sort of person, it's an incorrect interpretation. What would be the correct interpretation? The absolute complete interpretation of you? You are a child of God and I'd better not mess around with you. You see, if I'm angry with you I'm angry with the Light. And then, oh boy, I'll get into trouble. So—if I'm absolutely clean of any negative perception of you, I will see the Light. But as soon as I see you otherwise I'm shackling you. You can't get out of that. You're lassoed. You're now what

Hawaiians call 'a hostage of my thoughts.' You can't move."

According to the kahuna tradition we were all created perfect by the Light. But the Light gave us free will and in the course of many lifetimes we have chosen to move away from the Light. Consequently, today most of us are totally confused and lost. Yet because our essential nature is Light we are all capable of developing a personal relationship with Divinity and rediscovering our true perfection.

"For the Hawaiians it's very simple. In the beginning you were created perfect. Do you know

"There's nothing wrong with errors in thinking. They just kill you, that's all!"

what it means to be perfect? Perfect means that the very thought of you by the Light was Light. Because you were a reflection of the Light you were perfect.

"When you were this perfect being you were free. That's what love is. Love is to be free. You were born free and at that moment the Light said to you: 'I love you. And because I love you, you can stay with me or you can go.' Because that's what love is—no attachment. You were able to choose to be this or be that. And you chose, like me, to be 'that.' That's how it all started. And so, for whatever reason, you and Haleakala decided to go and move out of the Light. This has happened over more lifetimes than all the stars in the heavens. This is why we're loaded. We're ill. We get confused. We're in chaos all the time.

"You know, one day I was walking around the perimeter of the volcano. I live five miles from the most active volcano in the world. I was walking around the edges of it and heard this creaking sound. Creak... creak... creak... So I tuned in to the creaking sound and up came this person in this rocking chair.

A deity at the temple entrance of Pu'uhonua O Honaunau Natural History Park, on Big Island, Hawaii.

Rocking... rocking... So I asked this Being: 'What's happening?' The Being said: 'Well, I don't have anything to do and nobody talks to me.' That was the Light. Nobody talks to the Light. So that Light which created you is not very busy. Only busy making galaxies and that sort of stuff!

"I don't have to go to a guru or a priest. I can go directly to the Light. I like that. You don't have the wholesaler involved. You can go straight to the manufacturer. If you clear your mind the Divinity will talk to you directly, so you don't need books.

"The Light in Hawaiian is 'Ka I' (pronounced 'ka-ee'). You have to say it correctly because otherwise it means 'feces.' Like the word for the sunlight. If you mispronounce it slightly it means 'money.' That's how perceptive the Hawaiians were. The language had a great deal of metaphor!"

Haleakala teaches that the Light can only be experienced when our conscious mind turns toward our superconscious essence. It is by quieting the thinking mind and "not knowing," rather than through intellectual judgments, that we are able to be "in the void" and to avoid the "errors" in our thoughts which create all our problems.

A hula dancer and a conch-shell blower silhouetted against the Hawaiian sky at sunset.

Hawaiian canoes are long and narrow and need several rowers to propel the boat in the seas around the islands.

"People ask: 'What is the basis of life?' The scientists say it is DNA. For the Divinity the three aspects of your self is the essence of life. This 'Inner Family' is the key. Out of the Light comes the spiritual superconscious part of your being. It is always in connection with the Light. Why? Because it's perfect. At the next level is the mental part. The thinking part. What psychologists call 'conscious mind.' This is the part which manages. That can make choices. This is the important part because it can make the choice to be nurturing as opposed to being stuck in the intellect. And then there is the subconscious or the child. In this child is all the thought forms and all the memories. So when someone gets sad or angry it's just a repeat of something that has happened before.

"The only problem with human beings is that they are arrogant, because that's what thinking is. Thinking is in essence 'I know.' Wisdom is being in the void. To be thoughtless.

"Only by being in the void can the Light come through. As long as I have something going on in my mind the Light can't come through. The Light can only come in when the mind is cleared—in a state of silence.

"Our thinking becomes manifest in Mother Earth, so if we're angry we get weather in certain parts of the world which is man-made. I can't imagine that a just God would send down weather to kill people, can you? It has to be man-made. Something loving would not do that. So why are we killing ourselves and then blaming it on God?"

"The intellect is always trying to take a position and say: 'Here's what I am.' It can't help it. But you really don't know. The intellect just talks a good story. But does it produce results? I'm results oriented. The intellect has a magical ability to dance you. You get impressed. But you have to ask a very fundamental question. 'Show me! Give me results!' You can choose to be 'right' or to be peaceful. Being 'right' always leads to suffering."

Ho'oponopono means "to rectify an error." The practice of Ho'oponopono is about acknowledging that the problems in our lives are the results of "errors" in our thinking based on past memories. By realizing that we are entirely responsible for everything that happens to us, and repenting of our errors before the Light, the Light is able to transform our personal situation for the better.

"Today Ho'oponopono in Hawaii is just like family therapy. This has been really influenced by the Christians. But I'm talking about the real Ho'oponopono from before they came. Then the Hawaiians didn't need to talk to anyone. They could go straight to the Light. This is very ancient. It goes back to the start, because that's where Hawaiians came from.

A North Shore wave in the process of breaking.

The beautiful turquoise feathery leaves of the silversword (Argyroiphion sandwicense) on the Hawaiian island of Maui.

"The central point in Ho'oponopono is that all of the problems, stresses, and diseases that one experiences begin as replays of old negative emotional memories. Being residents of the cosmos, we all share in a common pool of old negative memories. Using the cleansing process of Ho'oponopono, one is able to petition the Light within to transmute old woes and replace them with divine peace. The key to the beginning of the cleansing process is self introspection. The question to be asked is: 'What is going on inside of me that is manifesting the problems?'

"If I'm angry that anger will manifest as cancer or something. If I want that cancer to go, all I have to do is shift my thought. And the way I do it is through a process of saying: 'I'm sorry. Forgive me for whatever is going on inside me that causes me to perceive that which is not working for anyone.' Once I say 'I'm sorry, please forgive me,' then the Light will actually shift that thought-form. Only the Light can do that. It will take anger and purify it and neutralize it. Then it will release it and there is nothing left there. The anger will disappear. And then it does something extra. Once there is release and an emptiness, the Light will then put in what is right for you.

"Ho'oponopono is a path of repentance and forgiveness. Before I can be forgiven I have to be repentful. You don't find too many people around here being repentful, because the opposite of repentance is blame. The opposite of being repentful and forgiving is not being 100% responsible. And without that I cannot make this cancer disappear. This is a manifestation of my thought. But if I shift my thought and allow it to be transmuted into Light, this thing will go. And when this thing goes, some new creation will come in. Through just being responsible the Light immediately gives you what you need and you'll be inspired."

In common with other shamanic traditions, the Hawaiian tradition teaches that all of life is interconnected. Ho'oponopono is, therefore, not only a way of healing ourselves, but others and our world as well. In fact, since we are all One we cannot fully heal our-

"The only question is whether we are going to choose to go home—to go back to the Light—or whether we are going to suffer."

selves except by healing everyone. Haleakala is a man who only values results and he claims that the ancient spiritual practice of Ho'oponopono can work miracles. He attributes to Ho'oponopono his success as a psychologist working with the criminally insane.

"We all have to move together. If you don't move, I can't move. If you don't go home, I can't go home. If you're not in the Light, I can't be in the Light. It's all for one and one for all. I can either go home with all of you, or I can't go home at all. It can't be done individually. But individual responsibility is important because it begins the process.

"You are in me and I am within you. You and I share all the common memories since the beginning of creation. Why is that so? Because we are like everything in a pot of stew. We can't escape each other. If someone calls me with a hip problem, I know it's caused by a memory. Because I share a common memory with that person, when I do this process called Ho'oponopono the memory will be transmuted. The way it works is I will say:

Lanikai Beach and the Mokulua Islands on the windward side of Oahu, Hawaii.

61

Palm trees typically fringe the beaches of the Hawaiian islands.

'I'm sorry, please forgive me,' and that sends it to the Light. And the Light sends down a transmuting vibration which shifts things back into Light and healing happens.

"No one wanted the job I did with the criminally insane. They were averaging about one psychologist a month. But I got asked. We had about 25-30 people. Half of them would be in shackles at the ankles or the wrists because they were dangerous. They could either kick you or slam you. Everyone would walk with their back toward the wall so that they wouldn't get struck. They had no family visits. No one could leave the building. A year and a half later there was none of that. There were people going out on bus rides. Nobody in shackles. The level of medication dropped. What did I do? I worked on myself. I took 100% responsibility.

"You never know what the Light will give you to do. The Light may say: 'OK the game's over.' I'm not here for the next lifetime. I'm here to get it over with. I see life as a process of being responsible and constantly clearing away 'errors.' And then man is able to evolve along with Mother Earth, the planets, a speck of dust, your shoes, this jacket—everything moves. I don't see myself as a kahuna. I see myself as a garbage collector. I'm only here to be responsible and it's often very hard to do that."

This method called the "Indigo Bowl" can help solve problems of any kind. It is best performed twice a week before retiring at night. Imagine placing all of your problems—to do with your self, your family, friends, ancestors, cars, pets, animate or inanimate things—into an indigo bowl, which is suspended over the center of the crater of the Haleakala volcano in Hawaii. Allow whatever you have placed in the bowl to turn from indigo to ice blue, and finally to white. Then the Divinity will finish the treatment and the situation will change.

LAMA KHEMSAR RINPOCHE
TIBETAN YUNGDRUNG BON TRADITION

Yungdrung Bon, meaning "Eternal Light", is the original spiritual tradition of Tibet. In fact, Yungdrung Bon sources claim it to be one of the oldest spiritual traditions in the world dating back 18,000 years to its founder Tonpa Shenrab Miwoche. Lama Khemsar Rinpoche is a Tibetan Lama of the Yungdrung Bon tradition whose own monastery is Pungmo-Gon in South Tibet. When the Chinese occupied his country in 1959, however, he sought refuge in India along with H.H. the Dalai Lama, the spiritual leader of Tibet. He is now the Spiritual Director of the Yungdrung Bon Study center in Britain of which he is the founder, the only center of its kind in Europe.

Lama is a Tibetan name for a spiritual teacher. Some lamas achieve this status through their own effort in this life. Others are reincarnations of past masters. Others still hold a family lineage. Lama Khemsar Rinpoche's family have been lineage-holders in the Wangden Zhu lineage of the Yungdrung Bon tradition for many generations, so he is a lama by birth as well as through extensive spiritual training.

Lama Khemsar Rinpoche's vision is to preserve the Yungdrung Bon tradition and make its ancient wisdom available to the West. As well as profound teachings of enlightenment Yungdrung Bon also incorporates many shamanic practices concerned with maintaining a harmonious relationship with the nagas or spirits. Lama Khemsar Rinpoche combines the roles of shaman, healer, astrologer, and spiritual guide. With his spacious presence and lilting voice this gentle Tibetan master seems to embody the indiscriminate compassion for all beings which he preaches.

In the Lama, Enlightened Ones, Teachings, and Spiritual
Warriors, I seek refuge until the attainment of enlightenment.
To liberate all the sentient beings, who are as one's Mother,
from the ocean of suffering, I generate in myself
the Sublime Mind of enlightenment.

May all the sentient beings that are encompassed by the
sky be enriched with happiness and the cause of happiness.
May all sentient beings be parted from suffering
and the cause of sufferings.
May all sentient beings be never parted from the
happiness of that nonsuffering state.
May the mind of all sentient beings abide in the state of
equipoise parted from both suffering and nonsuffering.

YUNGDRUNG BON PRAYER

65

Listening to Wisdomkeeper Lama Khemsar Rinpoche

A statue of Virudhaka, which acts as guardian of the southern town of Gyangze in Tibet.

"I am a Tibetan Bonpo Lama. We have five great families who have kept the lineage of the Yungdrung Bon tradition from the beginning—from the founder Tonpa Shenrab Miwoche. I am a lineage-holding Lama from one of these families. I'm originally from South Tibet. At the age of five I was first introduced to Tibetan reading and writing, and introduced to receiving empowerment and transmission according to the Bon tradition from one of the highest lamas in South Tibet. After having certain teachings and empowerments from different lamas in Tibet, I had to escape to India in 1959 along with His Holiness the Dalai Lama and other Tibetans. We Tibetans joined hands to build Bonpo culture and tradition in India. Here I continued my spiritual practice under many masters, including one of my root masters who died in 1985, who has now reincarnated back again. So we have a little boy who is six years old supposed to be the reincarnation of my root master."

"It is very important to restore the broken relationship between human beings and the spirits. Those spirits that reside in trees, grass, water, springs, lakes. Even in the sky, the clouds, everywhere."

Although Tibetan Buddhism is now extremely well known in the West, the Yungdrung Bon tradition is less familiar. It is a broad and highly sophisticated spiritual tradition, of which shamanic practices form an important part.

"The whole teachings of Yungdrung Bon is not shamanic, but it is a part within it. The whole Yungdrung Bon teaching is fully enlightened teaching. Yungdrung Bon—Eternal Light—is not a religion. It's a spiritual tradition meant for all sentient beings, including mankind. It has its own founder Buddha, Tonpa Shenrab Miwoche, whose history goes back 18,000 years. He was born in the land of Wölmolungring or Shambhala. All his teachings are based on indiscriminate love and compassion; treating every sentient being as one's father, mother, sister, and brother.

"Tonpa Shenrab Miwoche taught 84,000 teachings as an antidote to the 84,000 passions that we consist of. They are all summarized into the Nine Sequential Vehicles of Yungdrung Bon or simply the nine ways of Bon. Yes. Within these nine

Nomadic herders at the Karo La Pass area, near Yamdrok Yamtso Lake, on the boundary between Front and Back Tibet.

ways of Bon we have renunciation path, we have transformation path, we have liberation path. The ultimate aim of all these different parts within the Nine Vehicles is to get freedom and liberation from the suffering world. To get enlightenment.

"Now within the Nine Sequential Vehicles four are called 'Causal Bon' and four are called 'Resultal Bon' and the ninth one is the Liberation part. Within the

Causal Bon we have shamanic rituals, arts, healings, medicines, dealing with nagas or spirits. Yungdrung Bon is very, very rich in teachings for dealing with nagas. All these things can be termed a shamanic system. Therefore the whole thing in Yungdrung Bon is eternal enlightened teaching within which we do have a shamanic tradition, the aim of which is to liberate every sentient being to the enlightenment path."

According to Lama Khemsar Rinpoche's tradition, Yungdrung Bon was once taught all over the world. This explains its similarities with other shamanic traditions, such as those of the Mongolians, Australian Aboriginals, and Native Americans. Not only does it predate Buddhism in Tibet, but Bonpos see Buddhism as a later development of their own ancient tradition. They claim that, in a previous life, Shakyamuni, the founder of Buddhism, was actually a disciple of Tonpa Shenrab Miwoche, the founder of Bon.

"Yungdrung Bon is the original spiritual tradition of Tibet. It is also the cultural heritage of all Tibetans. There is nothing that is not connected with Yungdrung Bon tradition within Tibetan culture. Nothing. It is the original Tibetan teachings until we had Buddhism from India. Since then we have two spiritual traditions in parallel—the enlightened teachings of Tonpa Shenrab Miwoche and Tonpa Shakyamuni.

A village near Yamdrok Yamtso Lake, Tibet's third largest lake, situated at an altitude of 14,700 feet.

Local inhabitants and animals mingling in a Tibetan village.

"There are many similar teachings and traditions and concepts between Yungdrung Bon and Buddhism. But at the same time it has a different history. According to our sources the Yungdrung Bon was taught all over the world. In fact the texts say 'all over the universe.' The teachings declined in many many parts. But there are still traces of Yungdrung Bon teachings in countries like Mongolia, Afghanistan, Persia—even Australia, Native American. Everywhere we can find traces.

"But the teachings remained intact in Tibet. It was introduced there at a very late stage —about 3,000 years ago. Yungdrung Bon originated from the land of Zhang-Zhung, a neighboring country which is not existing today in name. Part of western Tibet used to be Zhang-Zhung. It was a huge country. It used to be an independent country. It had its own language and king. In those days Yungdrung Bon was very much flourishing in that land, while in Tibet there was no enlightened teachings as such. Tibet used to be called 'The Dark Land.'

"According to Yungdrung Bon sources the Buddha Shakyamuni the founder of Buddhism, who was born in India, was in fact in his past life a disciple of the founder of Yungdrung Bon tradition —Buddha Tonpa Shenrab Miwoche. At that time Buddha Shakyamuni he was called 'Son of sublime God with a crystal crown.' And after completing his studies under Tonpa Shenrab Miwoche he was entrusted to manifest in India and teach his Yungdrung Bon there as Dharma. So there is a connection in this way between Yungdrung Bon and Buddhism. We Bonpos highly regard Buddhism."

The shamanic or Causal teachings of Yungdrung Bon are largely concerned with the unseen nature spirits or nagas. Fundamentally they are of two sorts—enlightened and unenlightened. The former are

The characteristic red robes of Tibetan Buddhist monks, who have gathered together at Sarnath.

allies of human beings, while the latter can be danger-
ous if not appeased through shamanic rituals.

"'Naga' is a Sanskrit word which means serpent. But I don't think there is an appropriate translation in English. Nagas are the unseen spirits. In Tibetan we call them 'sadak-lu-nyen.' 'Sadak' literally means landowner. Nagas are the owners of the land, nature, the trees, the water, the earth, and so forth. Our shamanic naga rituals are to bring healing to them. To bring them to terms with human existence. To make a compromise between these unseen creatures or spirits and human beings. To harmonize human existence with natural existence.

"Under the terms nagas or sadak-lu-nyen there are many different categories. If I divide them into two, there are enlightened nagas and there are unenlightened nagas—just like there are enlightened and unenlightened sentient beings. So, for instance, when people want to make bridges, want to make roads, and they blast up rocks, cut forests, and disturb lakes, they are disturbing the existence of the nagas—their habitats. We are destroying and harming them. Shaking their cities. As a result of this the unenlightened nagas, because they are unenlightened, are angered. So they send their negative spirits toward the human beings who harmed them. And this also affects others. As a result of that we believe

The snow leopard or ounce, with irregular rosettes of large black spots,
is native to the mountains of central Asia.

that diseases, such as cancer and other kinds of disease, come from this. Therefore to negotiate with them, to appease these harmed nagas, we have very rich shamanic rituals and rites, and medical and folk remedies.

"The other nagas are enlightened nagas who are teachers. Instead of harming sentient beings or having negative thoughts they always help sentient beings. Some of these nagas give wealth—spiritual wealth, material wealth, and physical health wealth, mental health wealth. They always support in bringing awareness within sentient beings and look after their well-being. So there are, mainly speaking, these two different kinds of nagas."

Like many other shamanic traditions, Yungdrung Bon teaches that in truth everything is only an illusory projection of the mind. So, ultimately,

"We should perform our body actions, speech actions, thought actions with mindfulness while understanding the law of cause and effect. And always try to dedicate ourselves toward doing wholesome deeds, rather than unwholesome deeds. This is our great shamanic way of healing. Yes. This is my message."

nagas have no real existence. But neither does anything else! Relatively speaking, however, nagas are very real and have a powerful effect on human life. Although generally unseen, nagas do manifest in physical forms and can be directly experienced.

"Yungdrung Bon teachings are based on two truths. Ultimately nothing is existing substantially because everything is impermanent. There is no substantial existence as such. So in the ultimate truth everything is a projection of mind—including nagas. But in the causal way, in the relative way, nagas do exist. If somebody has a true love and caring toward these beings then he will have experiences of nagas. If we understand that, just as we like happiness and don't like suffering, also these existences like happiness not unhappiness. And we respect their existence. If someone wanted to experience the nagas just for fun or fantasy—I don't know about that.

"We have many stories of experiences with nagas in Tibet. Although we call them invisible spirits, nagas always manifest. They can manifest in different forms—serpent, snakes, frogs. Actually these serpent snakes are called nagas' messengers. Not real nagas. Sometimes good nagas manifest into the form of beautiful girls. Yes. There are great legends about these things."

Nagas can also manifest in dreams. Unenlightened nagas who have been harmed in some way by humans are a source of diseases and other misfortunes, so the Yungdrung Bon tradition teaches that we must appease them by performing very specific shamanic rituals.

"It is called irrational, but I have directly experienced different kinds of nagas. For instance, when we came to India. We had nothing. We left everything in Tibet. We had no source of income. So many problems. My father, for our living, bought a cow. From this one cow we developed to a dairy farm of 10 or 20 cows. My father used to say: 'This cow is naga manifestation.' And we didn't know what he meant to say. But later we could see that

Yaks, the traditional Tibetan beast of burden,
below the North Face of Pangma.

The Tibetan Himalayas: Guari Sankar seen from Menlungtse.

there was really something different about this cow. He meant to say this is a wealth-bringing naga. Since we had this particular cow, the numbers of the cows started increasing. The product went well in the market. So we said this is naga related.

"Sometimes if within the family there was a particular problem with sores on the body, cuts, infectious diseases, then this cow used to come into the dreams of my mother. And my mother would say: 'Oh, we should do some naga ritual because we are shown this cow.' It's not because of this cow. She is representing the nagas. And it's true. If you do these naga rituals the infectious diseases, these sores on your face, scabies, eczema, and other things, lung diseases, things like that, will heal.

"The idea is we might have done something to harm the nagas and we do the shamanic naga ritual to appease them. It is not necessarily us harming the nagas, but also our neighbors. We had Nepalese local people and they do all sorts of things like barbecues, which is against the nagas.

"Everyone of heart on this planet must respect the existence of every being. Not only human beings, but other beings."

Barbecue is a very harmful form because the burning meat and smell affects the existence of the nagas. It really intoxicates and puts them off. And when they are sick we are sick, because we're connected. But once we performed the naga rituals my mother had the dream again. This cow comes speaking and transforms into a wonderful girl. And my mother said: 'Ah, it worked. It's done.' Nagas appear in dreams as many things."

Today in the West we are not aware of the nagas, but in Tibet maintaining a harmonious relationship with these unseen beings is an essential part of ordinary life.

"In Tibet every house has a Lu-khang or 'naga palace' built next to one's house on a selected spot. It is always respected. It is a sanctuary, reserved, pure, unexploited. And every year a lama would come and perform the necessary naga rituals so that it keeps out all the harmful diseases for the family and brings spiritual and material wealth. To keep a respectful relationship with the spirits is very important.

"Naga rites and rituals are about rejuvenating and harmonizing the relationship between human beings and other beings. Yes. Because all of us, not only Tibetans but all human beings, had a spiritual bond from the very beginning with the other inhabitants on the planet. But we have lost this. We have forgotten, in the name of greed, anger, jealousy, wants. For us it's money, money, money, that is important. As a result we have turned a blind eye toward the nagas and their natural existence.

"For instance, today if we want to build a house or buy a house we just negotiate between the owner of the house and our self. And when that deal is done we then think: 'Well, the deal is done.'

A Tibetan dwelling in the village of Tingri.

Tibetan women drawing water at a well in the middle of a field of oil-seed rape.

According to Yungdrung Bon tradition, to build a house we have to negotiate with the beings to whom the place really belongs. No matter how high it is. Even if it is to be a monastery or palace of the Buddha. No matter how important the building is, we have to make payments to the nagas. We must first negotiate a deal with the original owner of the land. The spirits.

"So we have appeasing and resettlement of these inhabitants in a very peaceful way. We have different kinds of shamanic rituals. We cannot underestimate their existence if we want to flourish. This is important. If I want to build a house today, before doing anything, what we do is first go there and perform the necessary shamanic rituals and arts and things. To speak in simple language, we talk to the nagas. We say: 'I am here. I want to build a house here or a temple here. This is for the benefit of beings or for my living. I know this is your inhabitance here. With the power of the spiritual, with the power of the blessing, I respect you and I will rehabilitate you. Please let us do this.'

"We rehabilitated them, and only after that do we feel we have really done the negotiations with the real owner. And then we start building. We bring a lama who has really been endowed with true compassion of mind, who treats every sentient being with loving kindness, to come and use the first pickaxe. And we start building on an auspicious day, so that it doesn't harm anybody on this earth. These are the naga rituals and real shamanic things in Yungdrung Bon."

Lama Khemsar Rinpoche does not see modern science as in opposition to the ancient spiritual tradition of Yungdrung Bon, but as a potential coworker in the great human endeavor of relieving suffering. Science, for example, is very good at dealing with the symptoms of diseases. Yungdrung Bon, however, can see beyond the symptoms to the root cause of illness. The root cause is related to karma and a problem with the nagas. Only when this is healed through the necessary shamanic rituals can the source of the illness be healed. Then any form of medicine will be effective.

"I think Yungdrung Bon teachings are very relevant today. I think the collective ego of our scientists stops us looking into these things. But everything is there. Millions of dollars could be saved for humanity if we combined both science and the spiritual aspect together. I think both spirituality and science have great things to offer each other. For us science is actually a spiritual thing if

A nomadic musician and puppeteer in the Lhasa River valley—Kahm traders from eastern Tibet are distinguished by having their hair wound in cockscombs of yarn.

it is done in a proper way, because we can see so many great things in science which can really help in revealing the true essence of the spiritual side. But they must not contradict each other. They must come to a negotiation table. Come together, walk together, for the benefit of every being, with the right intent.

"For instance, science has done very fascinating things—treating human beings with different methods of medicines. But we understand that what is lacking in modern medical science is that they are just looking into the symptoms, which is secondary cause. The Law of cause and effect is one of the main subjects in our teachings. We are all accountable for what we do and what we did.

Plowing and sowing the land in the vicinity of Lhasa.

This is the root cause of our sufferings, which must be purified first.

"In science there is no understanding of the root cause. They know about a virus, keeping clean, healthy hygienic laws—which is great. In the West people take a shower every day in the name of hygiene and brush teeth. And keep the environment clean. Food clean. Must be very, very clean. But there are people in the world, in Nepal, in India, in Tibet, who have one shower once a year! Very rarely brush their teeth. Don't do anything. But they have no diseases such as AIDS and cancer and tuberculosis and dangerous things. They are the healthiest persons. Why? Because they don't have the root cause to have these cancers and diseases. You have these cancers here even though you are taking great care of your health, because you have never even thought about the root cause. So root cause is most important.

"For instance if you are treating cancer here in hospital today, you have different methods of treating which is very good. But I would say it is only secondary cause that you are treating. You must do a naga prayer, naga ritual, naga rectification, and appeasing first. Then you are released from the source of the problem. Sources must be cured first. As soon as sources are cured then you can use any medicine and they will work. This is what I am trying to do. This is my tradition."

The dramatic approach to Mount Everest,
the highest mountain in the world.

ANDY BAGGOTT
CELTIC TRADITION

Andy Baggott is a Celtic shaman and healer. Like many westerners who have been drawn to Shamanism his life has been an inspiring story of spiritual awakening. In his twenties he followed a conventional modern lifestyle, working as a general manager of pubs, restaurants, and nightclubs. In one short period, however, Andy's life collapsed around him. He lost his job and his company house, and his marriage broke up leaving him to care for his disabled epileptic young daughter, Lara. Through the transformative impact of these personal disasters, his true calling became clear to him.

Lara had begun having seizures after a bad reaction to a whooping cough vaccination, and it was her illness that triggered Andy's exploration of alternative medicine. He studied many different world traditions, including acupuncture, traditional Chinese medicine, and cranial sacral therapy. He eventually merged all these therapies with his growing understanding of his native tradition of Celtic Shamanism.

He experimented with his healing techniques on himself, and when he was happy with the results tried them on Lara. At one point she was having up to twenty fits a day, with fits occasionally lasting up to an hour and half. Today she is down to a few short fits a month, is completely free of medication and lives a happy and fulfilled life. Through the journey of transforming his own life and healing his daughter, Andy has developed the shamanic skills which enable him to help heal and transform others.

Andy's understanding of Shamanism has been shaped by many traditions, but it is his indigenous Celtic tradition which he feels is the ground from which he works. Although often regarded as a "dead" tradition, for Andy Celtic spirituality is still very much alive.

I call upon the four winds,
Earth to ground me,
Air to teach me,
Fire to empower me,
Water to uplift me.
I honor Grandmother Earth who bore me,
Grandfather Sky who watches over me,
And the Creator whose spark
Is within me and all things.

CELTIC INVOCATION

A barn owl alighting on a fence post at dusk.

"For me Shamanism is an attitude toward life more than a philosophy or a religion. It's running your life with respect and interaction—very much an Earth-based way of working. The system I use I would call Celtic, although it draws from the wisdom of Native American, Chinese, Wicca, and all sorts. You can learn from all things, because wisdom is wisdom. The truth is the truth.

"Celtic Shamanism has survived. There are folk healers and wise women still in Wales, Scotland, Cornwall, and in the West Country of England. These people work in the old ways and live by the land. And a lot of the knowledge is still accessible. I think in many ways it's brilliant that nothing has been written down—that there is no tenet of scripture. Because anything that is written down is open to interpretation and can become a doctrine. I believe that everybody's spirituality is their own."

The room in which Andy works with his patients is full of intriguing talismans and shamanic medicine tools—feathers, bones, stones, drums, and so on. These, he explains, are reminders of the teachings he has received from different animals and forces of nature, which reconnect him to these "energies."

"The whole of nature teaches by example and as human beings the best way to teach is by example. One of the things I always say to my patients is: 'You cannot change the world or those around you. You can only change yourself.' But as you change, just by example you change those around you. All this business of standing up and trying to change other people and nagging other people about their bad habits just doesn't work. The only way you can change other people is by changing yourself. And you do this by learning through example. That's what all these animal artifacts are about. They are animals I have interacted with and learned some of their characteristics by their example.

"I was working with owl medicine, for example, and everywhere I went I would find owl feathers. I was walking in the woods and found an owl wing that had obviously come from some predatory kill. And so I knew the owl was calling me and had something to teach me. I wore the feathers and meditated with owl feathers around me. I tried to be as much around owls as possible. What I learned from the owl was discernment, because at that time I was not judging those around me correctly. I was not accessing their characters well. My interaction with the owl gave me vision in the darkness so I could see people clearly. People could no longer upset me because I could recognize exactly where they were at.

"I have the cure to all diseases—You."

"All of the animals that I have artifacts of are animals who have taught me something—through observation of their behavior and spending time being close to their DNA. I certainly find that wearing feathers, holding bones, meditating with bones and things like that, helps me to gain more insight. I feel that at some level an animal's DNA has its own vibratory rate, like everything else in the universe, and by holding that artifact you can actually tune into that vibratory rate and see things from the animal's perspective."

Shamanism may be powerful, but power can corrupt. Andy teaches that Shamanism is a spiritual path not a way of accumulating personal power. The misuse of power is a constant temptation to the shaman, which makes the shamanic path potentially hazardous to those not properly grounded and free from egotism.

"You need to be grounded to get into touch with spirituality or else it's dangerous. Shamanism is very, very dangerous potentially. It is also potentially powerful. Anything that has the power to heal has the equally opposite power to harm. It's the law of the universe. It's the law of opposites. This is why the drugs used in western medicine have such horrendous side effects. They make symptoms dramatically disappear but at the same time they do damage.

"Shamanism, if practiced responsibly with an open and pure heart and with a complete loss of ego, is safe and very, very powerful. And can create dramatic change both in the practitioner's life and in the patients' lives. But equally, because you have a certain amount of power when you work shamanically, that power can corrupt. There are plenty of people who allow that power to corrupt and you get tempted all the time. It's a matter of having that clarity of mind. It's so important to be responsible in Shamanism—not using that power to manipulate people to your own ends. I certainly use my power to manipulate people because I have people come to me who are very weak and disempowered, and I utilize my power initially to focus them in on what needs to be done. But the moment I see them gaining their power, that's when I step back."

For Andy, the role of the shaman is to empower the people he helps. We become empowered by changing the way we think and accepting responsibility for all that happens to us.

"I regard myself as a medicine man. I work on people and help people physically, emotionally and spiritually. But the whole of the emphasis is on personal empowerment. Every individual should be able, if they want to, to eat in harmony with their environment and be free from all illness. To not need western medical intervention in their lives. To live happy, fulfilled, and healthy lives until such time that they want to disincarnate. To live according to the laws of the universe. That destiny is available for everybody.

"From my perspective we are responsible for absolutely everything that happens to us. You attract everything that

happens to you. If you walk out and get run over by a drunk driver it's your fault, because if you are truly walking in harmony your own senses would warn you of danger.

"The idea of life is to learn lessons and obviously the more lessons you learn the wiser you become, and the more spiritually evolved you become. Then you can help more people. This is an ongoing procession through many incarnations. What Shamanism does is that it helps me find solutions to problems and to learn lessons. If in this normal reality of a western world I am presented with a problem that I cannot solve, then I go and commune with nature. That changes my consciousness and my thought patterns, and solutions that I hadn't seen with my western consciousness suddenly become apparent.

Glastonbury Tor, Somerset, England.
An ancient center of "Celtic spirituality."

"So one of the fundamental things about Shamanism for me is this changing your thinking pattern; changing the way your mind works. You need to get from unhealthy thinking to healthy thinking, where you live in the present and the past is just a memory. You put the past into perspective and you learn your lessons from it. And you look forward to the realization of your dreams and your destiny before you."

Andy teaches that "we are what we eat." A healthy diet is the secret to a full and satisfying life. By only eating the foods that grow in our environment we can stay in harmony with the natural world around us.

"Shamanism is about having a close interactive relationship with the whole of creation. And, therefore, whatever you find in creation that's what you have to align yourself to. If you want to communicate with a tree, then you stand a much better chance of doing that if everything going into you is in harmony with the season. If you start eating citrus fruit, tropical fruits, sugars, and things like that, and you go up to an oak tree in England—your whole vibration is completely different.

"We are not eating in harmony with our climate and the seasons. That means that our biochemistry is off balance. Also the amount of

The Black Rock Nature Reserve, in the Mendip Hills in Somerset, photographed in December.

"Every single negative has a positive side and you've just got to find it, and Shamanism helps you do that."

The common or red fox, native to Britain, is primarily a nocturnal animal and is rarely seen during the day.

chemicals and toxins that are in the food chain now is just so horrendous. And all the toxins have this effect of ungrounding you. If you want to be a spiritual being the more grounded you are the higher the realms you can get to. From my experience it works exponentially. The most fundamental thing to being able to cope with Shamanism is being grounded, because if you have visions they can be really quite scary if you've not got your feet firmly on the ground.

"You are what you eat. If you sort out your nutrition, then everything else sorts out and you can be happy, fulfilled, and healthy. It's so simple and that's why it's so powerful. There are certain foods that are fundamentally bad—sugar being the number one food. If you actually take sugar cane and suck it, you will find you can only suck it for a very short time because it's too sweet. But once you refine it, suddenly it becomes much less sweet and highly addictive. In the same way in South America a tribesman will pick a single coca leaf and put it under his tongue and chew it for suste-

nance on a long journey, but you cannot take too many because they are so bitter. Your body's natural taste buds turn around and say: 'Look, you've had enough of this.' But if you take many thousands of coca leaves and extract cocaine—suddenly your taste buds have got no taste for when they have had too much.

"Cocaine and sugar are very similar in their addictive nature and their disempowering nature. Three and half ounces of sugar will weaken your immune system by 50%, simply because it

A rabbit on the lookout in a wildflower meadow.

takes so much energy for your pancreas to produce insulin to bring your blood sugar level back down. And all the time your body's energy is doing that it cannot be feeding your immune system."

Andy helps his patients by modifying their diets so that their bodies can naturally heal themselves. He also undertakes shamanic journeys to find new solutions to their problems. But he does not see illness as a negative experience. It is a great teacher which can play an important role in our spiritual evolution.

"Nutrition is fundamental to our very existence. I have patients worldwide who come to see me with problems that doctors can't treat. And the majority of the work I do is getting them into balance and harmony with their environment.

"I have a lot of patients coming to me who are at their wits' end. I had a nineteen-year-old girl coming to me covered in eczema. Another women came to me from Singapore with irritable bowel syndrome because all they wanted to do was put her on tranquilizers. It took only a few days with the right nutrition to get her pain-free. For people who follow what I teach I have 100% success rate—about 90% actually do. After two weeks the girl with the eczema was virtually cleared, just through detoxing, clearing out her system, getting her to eat in harmony with her environment, rebalancing her blood sugar levels, and allowing her body to heal itself.

Pollarded willows along a riverbank in the Somerset Levels, England.

"Sometimes patients come to me with problems and I cannot find a solution in the physical. I've tweaked their diet, but nothing is changing. So then I travel shamanically—sometimes with them, sometimes without them. I travel shamanically and try and solve the problem. When you see things from a different perspective, that's when you find solutions.

"Illness is your body's way of trying to teach you something. The reason people keep getting ill is that they are not learning lessons. Pain can teach great things. Illness can be a great teacher. But it's not for me to say you need to do this because I know it will make you healthy. Maybe you have great lessons to learn from ill health. I'm a firm beliver that everything has its time and its place. If you have an open heart then everything is right. There are no mistakes, only lessons. If you can have that attitude it makes life an adventure."

"If you put the energy out for a dream, then you can draw in the connection you need to make that dream reality. Write down your wish on a piece of paper. Get into a quiet space and put all of your intent into your wish. Then burn the piece of paper sending the wish out to the universe, using the power of fire and smoke to carry that wish. Then you have to trust everything that is coming to you is coming to teach you and help to facilitate that wish— good or bad."

AIKO AIYANA
SANTO DAIME TRADITION

In 1922 Raimundo Irineu Serra, a Latin-American of African descent, was twenty years old. Strong and almost seven feet tall, he became a rubber tapper in the Amazon jungle. This brought him into contact with Peruvian shamans who used the power plant ayahuasca to produce a potent tea that induced visionary states. Although brought up a Catholic, Irineu studied with these shamans. Following instructions given to him in a vision, Irineu journeyed deep into the heart of the rain forest, where for eight days he drank only ayahuasca. By the fourth day he was having continuous visions of a female figure who called herself "Our Lady of Conception, the Queen of the Forest." She imparted to Irineu a spiritual doctrine in which drinking the sacred ayahuasca tea was to be the central ritual—a natural Eucharist.

Inspired by his vision Master Irineu founded Santo Daime, an extraordinary synthesis of Amazonian Shamanism with Catholic Christianity. The Queen of the Forest was portrayed as identical with the Christian Virgin Mother, and the saints' days of the church were adopted as holy festivals of the new shamanic religion. In visionary states Irineu received over a hundred hymns, which form part of what is regarded as a Third Testament of Christ.

In the early 1980s, after Master Irineu's death his successor, Padrinho Sebastião Mota de Mota, created a Santo Daime community in the jungle where initiates could practice their faith in peace. Based on Master Irineu's spiritual and environmental principles this remarkable community flourished and has became the center of an international network of Santo Daime churches.

Aiko Aiyana has been an initiate of the Santo Daime church for over nine years and is authorized to facilitate Santo Daime ceremonies. She sparkles with enthusiasm for the sacred ayahuasca tea she calls simply "the Daime," which has transformed her life.

I am the shine of sun.
I am the shine of moon.
I give the shine to stars,
because they all follow me.
I am the shine of sea.
I live in the wind.
I shine in the forest,
because she belongs to me

SANTO DAIME HYMN

LISTENING TO WISDOMKEEPER AIKO AIYANA

"Santo Daime to me is a tool for self knowledge, in that shamanic way of showing you who you are; how to be better; how to eliminate certain things. Just refining and really understanding who I am. 'Santo' means 'holy' and 'Daime' means 'give it to me.' So it is the 'holy give it to me'! So you are asking for the sacred teachings.

"The name of the plant used is ayahuasca, but we never refer to it as that. The Indians have been drinking ayahuasca for years and years and years. Master Irineu started having rituals with the Indians—the people of the forest. And then he had a vision of the Goddess of the Forest. He fasted for

The spectacular Iguaçu Falls in Paraná state, Brazil, where the water plunges in 275 separate falls.

many days and then she reappeared and channeled the whole Santo Daime Doctrine. And he began spiritually receiving hymns, and all the basic symbols of the path came about. That was the beginning of Santo Daime in Brazil, and now it is all over the world—the States, Japan, Hawaii, Europe.

"With the Santo Daime, people have more of a spiritual experience than the pure shamanic use of ayahuasca. It's more devotional. Whereas in the other teachings it is more individual.

"When I was in the Amazon doing ayahuasca with a shaman I understood my mother was going to die, and I was shown certain things. I experienced visions of a black panther. Really quite wild visions. But in Santo Daime there is more of a sanctified holy sacred vibration. But I think other rituals with the same ayahuasca tea still receive the teachings. However it is not quite the same. The spirituality aspects are different. In Peru their ceremonies are more to do with Mother Earth. They are quite earthy. And the tea is quite different, because they have mainly the vine. Whereas in Brazil they have a lot of bush and vine. But in Peru the bush doesn't grow very well. So it's more vine, which is more 'yang'—harder; more 'male'—very physical. And they use it with other plants—datura and other plants. So it is different.

"Even though it is very Christian, Santo Daime has the shamanic elements of the sun and

A Xikrin Native of Brazil's Amazonia, wearing traditional headgear.

the moon, the stars, the forest, the sea, the mountains, the nature elements. There are different healing entities and spirits. Shamans can experience them directly and see these energies, these entities, at work. These spirits are everywhere. They don't have boundaries. You can find all the same forces in the city. Obviously, they are stronger in places where there is no electricity and it's not a concrete jungle. But spirits go anywhere. However when you go to the rain forest, you experience them much stronger there."

The Santo Daime ceremonies which Aiko and her husband lead are extremely structured religious events. Although the participants have all ingested a powerful psychedelic the atmosphere is one of order and concentration, with the singing of devotional hymns in Portuguese and an atmosphere of fervent prayer. Yet Aiko is not formal or "religious," but relaxed and natural. The formality of the ritual is not practiced for its own sake, but to help focus the spiritual potential of the Daime.

"Santo Daime is very structured and I like that. There's a certain discipline. I'm definitely a 'free spirit' type of person. However, in the ritual I

A Yanomani Native shaman taking Yopo
hallucinogenic snuff through a pipe.

really see that the form has a meaning. And perhaps parts of it are there to really shake up someone's resistance to discipline and authority, and to conforming. And by shaking that, it opens them up more to certain experiences.

"For every ritual, there is a certain meaning. And the longer I do it, the more I see the power of the hymns. And it's becoming that the hymns are coming through me and it's not even me singing them. I'm just the instrument and they are coming from another place. As you surrender to that light, the more you go on a journey.

"The sexual energies are separated in the doctrine of the Santo Daime. They are two very different energies, so it is much more powerful to keep these energies separate. In the rituals in Brazil there are three or four hundred people singing and dancing in lines. A men's line. Then across from them there's a women's. And then a virgin's line. And then solitary men, or virgin men, or men who have decided to be celibate. And all the lines dance. It's very powerful. In these works in Brazil there are guitarists and drummers, electric piano. It's really alive. It just fills you up."

Someone officially becomes a Santo Daime
initiate when the Padrinho or Madrinha, the spiritu-

"You can get blasted wide open.
And that is why it is so important when you do
this sort of work to have spiritual protection.
Because everything gets exposed for a
spiritual cleansing, spiritual purification."

al "father" or "mother," pins a star on them during their initiation ceremony. When you become an initiate you affirm that the Daime is your guide and master. As an initiate you are responsible for others in the spiritual family of seekers. Initiates all wear uniforms, which can seem strangely out of place in a ceremony centered on ingesting a shamanic power plant! But like so much in Santo Daime, outward appearances can be deceptive; inwardly such formality serves a spiritual purpose.

"It's been nine years since I took the uniform. What's the uniform about? Well, I had it explained to me that if you've got the uniform certain beings in the other world, they don't bother you because they recognize you're with the Santo Daime. They see the uniform and they just don't bother you. And when I first came to the uniform, this understanding helped me get through that.

"I remember this experience when I got my star in Brazil at an all night work. This was the festival of St. John the Baptist. I was told I could not rest for more than three songs. You have to be up working when you have a star. You work. You're there to help. It's spiritual work, not an experience you just sit down and have. You're there to develop your spiritual muscles. You're working to help other people. Creating like a passageway of light for all beings. And you're conscious of working the whole night. At midnight they gave me my star.

"Then in the second half of the work, I had the biggest clean-out. I must have emptied everything out. A bolt of lightning went through me. They helped me to be seated at the altar and I

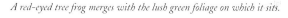

A red-eyed tree frog merges with the lush green foliage on which it sits.

could literally see the energy coming from the music and it was entering me. Just filling me with light. It was absolutely amazing. I was completely empty, with no energy, just bliss. Then this wonderful woman patted me on the shoulder and said: 'It's time to get back to work.'"

Bromeliads, plants of the pineapple family, in the Catac National Park in the Peruvian Andes.

The essence of Santo Daime is the healing and visionary experiences which the magical tea engenders. These experiences are transformative but not necessarily pleasant. Participants often undergo nausea and vomiting, but this is all seen as part of the cleansing process.

"My feeling is that what you are ready for happens. For people who have worked on themselves, maybe they feel a bit sick but they are able to understand why they feel sick. They cleanse it and then are able to really have a lot of incredible realizations. To have a positive experience you have to go through the resistance. And sometimes that's heavy. I've known people who have suffered incest and sexual abuse in their lives, and they've blanked it out. They've blocked it so they have no memory. And the first time they take the Santo Daime they see everything. It is a major thing in their lives which they have to heal before they can go forward.

"How you experience the Daime just depends on where you are at. I've had very difficult works. But when I look at the big picture, even when it's been bad, it's been really, really, necessary. I look at it in terms of my own evolution. But it's not all difficult. There is tenderness and joy and light. I would say that, in the traditional sense of Shamanism, you have to deal with the shadow. There is no denying the shadow. The shadow is part of the journey in all Shamanism. And what I

"In Peru they call ayahuasca the 'death vine' because you actually die to parts of yourself which don't serve you."

"My son Sienne has never been sick. When you get your star you can drink as much Daime as you like. But even when he got his star, no matter how much Daime he drank, he wasn't sick. He shakes the maraca and he sings. And he's been doing this from as soon as he was walking. He's shaking the maraca and doing the Santa Daime dance. So how can I deny him? When he first was asking, I didn't take him very seriously. But how can I deny this person who says: 'I want my star' at two years old! He's so committed to the path. He knows the melodies and the hymns, and he will sing along. You can't disturb him. Now he's got a star, a little children's star, he says: 'Mommy, I want to go to Brazil.' And that just roots you right where you are!"

Santo Daime is a doorway into the visionary world of the shaman. But for Aiko the important thing is to integrate the teachings received with day-to-day existence, and live with greater integrity and awareness.

"The problem with shamanic work is the question: 'How do you integrate it with your life?' It's fine to have an experience. But a lot of people

The black panther is simply a color variation of the leopard; its pattern shows up in a "watered silk" effect.

then do not bring the teachings into the physical, where there needs to be a grounding. It's great to go out and do shamanic work. To have all this stuff going on—out-of-body experiences and sensing different energies. But then what do you do with it? So I think that the real test is can you walk your talk in order to put the teachings into reality. And so I really try to integrate them into my life.

"The Daime is not for everyone. It's a gift for those who choose it—or for those who are chosen. It's a tool for those that are chosen. The Daime calls you. That's the reason why we don't invite anyone to come to the works. Because they've not been called."

MARTÍN PRECHTEL
TZUTUJIL MAYAN TRADITION

Martín Prechtel is an internationally respected shaman and healer. He is also the author of *Secrets of the Talking Jaguar: A Mayan Shaman's Journey to the Heart of the Indigenous Soul*, a powerful account of his remarkable life. He is half-blooded Canadian Native American and half-blooded Swiss. He was raised on a Pueblo Indian reservation in New Mexico where Shamanism was a living tradition and the only white man was his father. At the age of twenty, following a number of dreams, he ended up in the central highlands of Guatemala. He was drawn to a particular village where an old man picked him out of the crowd and announced: "I have been waiting for you for a couple of years. Let's go! Let's get to work!"

This old man was a Tzutujil Mayan shaman called Nicolas Chiviliu Tacaxóy and Martín became his apprentice. He stayed in the village as a practicing shaman for fourteen years, eventually rising to the office of Nabey Mam, first chief. In the mid 1980s Nicolas Chiviliu told Martín to return to the US and "plant" what he had learned. Today he works as a medicine man and teacher in North America and Europe, bringing the ancient ancestral wisdom of the Mayan people to the modern world.

In the Mayan tradition shamans are not saintly priests. They are rugged individualists who are treated with a mixture of awe and suspicion. The shaman is someone with a special intimacy with nature who can speak for the village community in the spirit world.

Martín is like a force of nature. There is a wildness at the very heart of his being which is challenging, inspiring, and direct. From his wealth of personal experience in a traditional village environment, he speaks of the spirits and the other world with a familiarity and forthrightness which fascinates and bewilders the logical mind. His vision of life and death has a raw and primal quality that confronts and confounds any cozy modern notions of what indigenous Shamanism might be.

Long Life
Honey in the Heart
No Evil
Thirteen Thank Yous.

MAYAN PRAYER

"In my tradition a shaman is called an Acjun, which means a person who goes looking. The most literal translation is 'hunter' or 'tracker.' In the village a shaman is what could be called an 'advocate' or a 'lawyer.' But he doesn't go between people. He intercedes on behalf of the human center of the village with the spirit world—which is kinda complex. It's not the simple-minded projection that most modern people have of what a native cosmology is. It's not so coarse. It's really fine. And because it's so fine there is no shaman who knows all of it. They all know a little bit of it.

"The difference between a shaman and a priest, and I am talking about a native priest, is that a priest does rituals on a regular basis throughout

"Most shamans are lame because they lean toward nature."

the year in order to maintain the village and the integrity with the spirits, and the balance between the amount of spiritual energy. Whereas a shaman is more a 'fix-it' man. They work with the same spirits. And they work in the same places and the same shrines. But the shaman is more allied to nature. The shaman is considered from nature, so the people are always a little suspicious of the shaman. They know he really is not working for the people. He is really more in love with nature.

"What the modern world calls Shamanism is not all Shamanism. For instance, we may say: 'Don't kill that ant because it did so and so in the old days' and 'This rock is sacred because it's where the ancestor lays his head.' But everyone in the village knows this, not just the shaman. But if you are not from the village this might seem like Shamanism. But the shaman goes further. He knows the sacred names of the rock and how to talk to it. How to go into it.

"Speaking well is important to the shaman, so that they can charm the spirits with offerings. Speaking eloquently in sacred ways is an offering. They can talk in such a way that touches the heart. This is also very important for the priests with their set liturgies, of course. The priests repeat things someone else learned a thousand years ago from the spirit world directly. But shamans are real individuals. There are woman shamans and hermaphrodite shamans. In fact, nearly all hermaphrodites are shaman. But a shaman is never a prophet or priest.

"The westerners have this idea that a shaman is a guru, but shamans are technicians. They are lovers of the sacred, but are no way looked upon as being exemplary. They are not 'holy men.' They are technicians of the holy. You'd never say to your kids: 'Grow up and become a shaman,' like you might say: 'Grow up and become a farmer.' It's like telling someone to be like a fighter pilot!"

Martín sees Shamanism as playing an important role in reconnecting westerners to their deep indigenous souls. But he urges caution on those with naive notions about the spirits who dabble with Shamanism. Being a shaman is a dangerous vocation which no one would voluntarily choose.

"Shamanism is of no use to the modern world. It's subversive of it. It's getting people back to their roots. When I returned to the US I didn't

Spring blossom and the peak of the Volcan Agua loom over Guatemala's former capital of Antigua.

want to teach. I mean, I lived in the bush. I would be riding for days. I had pet wolves. I was a terror. But I was invited to a men's conference and I was told: 'You don't have to teach if you don't want to.' But I went and what I saw really impressed me. And I felt really welcome because I realized these are the refugees from the western culture. And I realized we had something in common and therefore something to offer each other.

"Shamanism is not to be confused with entertainment—like people taking drugs and getting high. Shamanism says everything is alive. The spirits are alive. You really can't be naive about this. The problem with people that are dabbling around with so-called 'Shamanism' is that they think they can sit there on some hill that was used long ago for ceremonies, and take flowers and go up there and say to some unhappy spirit 'I love you,' and that that will make things OK. It's like going back to an

*The Quiche Maya Native vegetable market
at Chichicastenango, Guatemala.*

old girlfriend and saying: 'I've decided you are the most beautiful after all.' Well, the girlfriend you have abandoned a long time ago, she is not going to say: 'I knew you'd come back.' It will be like— 'Well! Hey sucker!' And then BAM! You get hit. And you have to be awake about this. That is what the shaman does. He is not naive.

"No one is simply trained to be a shaman. They have to be born for it. The spirits have to choose you. People say: 'You want to be a shaman? I want to be a shaman!' And it's like, 'Oh no you don't!' First of all you just can't do that. Like, in the village a little kid is born and the midwife is looking at him and checking out his body, and she might say: 'Oh this is one!' But you never notify the parents because they would just get depressed.

"Shamanic initiation is so strong it has to be done very gradually, because very often the ini-

tiate is destroyed and killed. I went through it. Two students that were being initiated with me died. I almost died too. So there's lots of preparation for initiation. You learn to go into the other world. You literally disappear. I disappeared and turned up in a lake! They tell you prayers, but they only give you the ends of them. And if you bring the beginnings back with you, then they know that you have understood. When you go into that trance place you have got to be careful because you may be going there to help someone, but you could also kill someone, because you really aren't meant to be flying around out there unless you've got a license. And you're not supposed to be flying around just for fun. It has to be useful."

Shamans heal by working in the other world to retrieve lost spirits, capture ghosts and make deals with the gods. But someone does not become a shaman simply by being initiated or by learning shamanic techniques. His reputation is built upon the results he achieves. The proof of his powers is that they work.

"Even when you are initiated you are just another guy in the village until you have proved yourself. Shamans are healers and your credentials are the number of people you have healed, not because you have come out of college with something that says you are good at something. If people don't get well you haven't got the stuff. The spirits are not listening. But if they do get well—

"The word for 'life' in Mayan means 'mutual indebtedness.' Everything is mutually indebted."

OK. My speciality was curing epileptics. People came from all over the country and I had about a 90% cure rate.

"In a village situation when a human is ill, rather like everywhere else, they take herbs and things like that, and think: 'I'll be better tomorrow.' But if they don't get better, then that is a sign of a bigger cause. So then it's generally looked upon that the human is not ill, but the spirit has got lost in another world. Or he has been attacked by a witch or something like that. So a shaman is called in to retrieve the spirit that got lost in the other world.

"If one person is sick then the whole family are looked upon as sick, because the whole family forms one body. Say cousin Ramon is sick, then they figure that the whole clan is ill. So whole people will come to the shaman. They won't send one guy. In fact the sick guy may not come at all,

Powerful roots support the native trees in the jungle at Tikal, Guatemala.

because he is sick. He'll stay at home. It's the other people who will come and say something is wrong. The shaman will determine what it is.

"A lot of times shamanic work is capturing ghosts. Alcoholics who have mental disturbances, for example. If they are not mourned properly when they die, if not enough tears are shed for them, there is not enough energy to get them to the Beach of Stars. Then they come back. Or if their trespasses are heavy. Heavier than the boat that is carrying them. Then they can't get over there. And since they haven't got a body anymore, they have to go and live with the tenderest member of the family. So the smallest or most beautiful child or the most magnetic child will be the one

Women from the Ixil tribe inspecting pots at Nebaj, Guatemala.

who will get this ghost. And they will start to suffer or go crazy. And you understand that the ghost is not bad. It just wants to stay alive. And when it has done eating that generation, it jumps to the next generation. And that person will develop the same problems. So the ghost is added to. So you get two ghosts, three, four, until he gets big and his hunger is bigger. So he has to eat more. So it starts eating whole situations. So what a shaman does is to come in and capture the ghost in a very concrete way. And you have to charm these ghosts. This works very well in the modern world too."

According to the Maya, the spirits feed us by creating the natural sustenance we need, but they in turn are dependent on us for "food." The shaman makes sure that the spirits get fed and are not driven to make raids on this world to satisfy their hunger, causing unintended misery and distress to human beings. The spirit world and this world are pictured like two wings. The shaman makes sure these two aspects of reality are working together in natural harmony.

"Mayans have so many deities but there is one major concept of a deity. It's called the 'Venerable Queen.' Humans have stolen her daughter for agriculture. And as long as we have been doing things—mining things out of the earth or changing things as they occur naturally—we have incurred a debt against nature. Then nature is not happy. So nature is like a mother-in-law who

A Pueblo house, traditionally made of adobe or earth bricks, in Taos, New Mexico.

we didn't ask to steal her daughter. Whatever bad that happens to someone in their daily life means that nature is taking back something. This is very different from western thinking.

"Usually the problem with the spirits is not that they are mad at you, but mainly because they are hungry. They are not looking for vengeance, so you can make some sort of a substitute. A shaman is someone who makes a good deal with the spirits. What Shamanism is all about is dealing with things when the integrity of the village has finally been compromised because the spirits have been forgotten. The priests are in charge of keeping the people in the state that they don't forget. But when that gets out of balance, for

whatever reason, then the shaman is called. The shaman is called because he knows how to deal with atypical situations. When nobody knows what to do, they call the shaman.

"He usually has two or three assistants. I used to be an assistant. You become like an anchor so that the shaman can go traveling into the other world and talk directly to the spirits—you might call them deities or gods. The gods live in another dimension and that dimension is dependent on this one. In truth they don't talk directly to the gods, except in certain cases. The shaman goes out as a scout and meets the deity's dogs. These dogs are

"The essence of getting near to the understanding of the shaman is, instead of seeing nature, see out of the eyes of nature. You see the world out of the eyes of a trout or a tree. There is a kind of grief and melancholy in human beings because of their inability for doing this. It's sort of beat out of us somehow."

not like the modern dogs—the domesticated dogs of the cities. These dogs are like very brave dogs in the village. They keep their master safe. So the shaman goes to the other world as a messenger and the gods would say: 'You know the humans have been taking a lot of deer recently and we are not being fed properly so we cannot produce properly.'

"You see, the spirits are not being fed properly and are being forgotten, but still life continues and they still make the fields fertile. So then they are forced to make raids and they are seen as forces of nature. And if you see an AIDS epidemic or a big boat sinking, that is the spirits having to take what they need. The energy which they need. The energy transfer. So when they are forgotten they have to come and take what they need or else they too will die."

The spirits feed us through the natural world all around us. We feed the spirits by offering them as gifts human artifacts, which the spirits are unable to create themselves. We need what the spirits give and the spirits in turn want what we have. When the spirits are forgotten this reciprocal relationship goes out of balance and the spirits become malevolent rather than benevolent forces in human life.

"The way you go about remembering the spirits is not just keeping them in mind. The way you remember them for the Maya is that they gave you everything you have got, so you've got to give them back something of what you create. You have to give them things that have been altered by human hands. For instance, you may give them flowers. Well, flowers come from the spirits. We didn't make the flowers. So we take them and make them into some mysterious shape. Or even shred them so that they come alive in the spirit world. We take beautifully made bowls and 'BANG!' We break them so they come alive on the other side. We make liquor, which the spirits do not know how to make, and we give it to them.

Luxuriant vegetation is a feature of the landscape near Tikal, Guatemala.

A peach-colored flower of the hibiscus, which grows mainly in tropical and subtropical areas, here native to Guatemala.

So they want not so much the material object as the gesture of making the gift.

"Words which accompanied the gifts are so important. The words themselves describe the gifts in such a way that they come alive in the other world. When we speak to the spirits beautifully they get drunk. So the shaman are like bartenders. They are the ones who make these beautiful gifts, and they give them to the spirits. The spirits do not have opposable thumbs, so the spirits cannot create things with their hands. Everything they see—beautiful things, bracelets—they say: 'Why don't we have anything like this?' So the Maya spirits want these things. So we give them jewelry and things.

"A funny thing happened. Well, it was not funny to my people, but it was funny to the outsiders. I was a chief at the time and all the big leaders came to me and said that the old guys were in deep discussion of a problem they had because of a keeper of one of the gods. The god had come to the keeper in a dream—because that is how you communicate with a deity if you are a regular person. This god was irritated because he had seen American tourists in the village who had sunglasses, and he had no sunglasses and he didn't know why the hell they were treating him like that. After all, he was a solar deity and he should have sunglasses! So they had come to the council to find out where they could buy them. So they went many, many miles to the big city and got piles of sunglasses. And to this day the deity has to have sunglasses. Now they are asking for watches and all sorts of things, because deities want what the humans have got.

"When the people don't give what the spirits expect, then they lose the balance. With all the things we make or fabricate we should have some consciousness of where we got the gifts from to make them. From the spirits who gave you the thumbs—although they themselves don't have them. It's like the goddess who allows women to have babies. She hasn't got any kids so she is very jealous of women that do. And they have to be very, very careful of them or else she will take them away to the spirit world where she is surrounded by children."

The price of human life is death, which feeds the spirits who made life possible in the first place. By seeking to heal someone who is dying the shaman interferes with this natural process and must be careful that curing one person does not simply compel the spirits to seek their sustenance from someone else's death. He therefore negotiates a deal with the spirits by offering them substitutes for the death of the ill person in the form of turkeys or other offerings and gifts. Eventually we all feed the spirits. The aim of spiritual initiation is to become a more worthy gift to the spirits, so that one's death benefits both gods and people.

"The function of the shaman can be very scary and people might think: 'Is he working for us or not?' If you get on the wrong side of a shaman you could be dead when you get up in the morning! He is a doctor. But if you want to cure someone of a sickness and the earth wants him to die, then the doctor is in trouble. If it's his time to go to feed the spirits, then you are taking the hors d'oeuvre out of the mouth of the very thing that is feeding the rest of the people. So how do you make it all right to save that person? And how do you know that by keeping him alive you are not killing someone else? So what the shaman does is that he tries to secure a sort of a loan in the form of

Women and children in the Holy Week procession in the village of Zunil, Guatemala.

turkeys and offerings and gifts. He gets to the spirits so they will receive those instead of this guy who is ill. Well, they are going to get this guy later anyway! So that's why the shaman is a kind of advocate or broker—a spirit broker.

"So the point is, if one is not giving those rents or payments then the spirits come to take them. And it's not because they don't like you. It's because they are starving—like a wild bear. The point is you have to take really good care of these spirits otherwise they are forced to start ravaging. And now when someone is being eaten by the spirits they don't try to feed the spirit. The spirit is

The plumed basilisk, a Central American lizard, has a well-defined crest on its head.

"Spirits are addicted to human beauty."

ravaging hungry but they try and kill it—give it Prozac or something. So the uses of Shamanism, at least in our tradition, is making sure that the spirits get fed.

"As you get older and go through all the layers of initiation you become a more and more worthy thing. Your death is a great and wonderful gift of food to the spirits. Being old and dying heavy is a great thing. When my teacher died the earth shook and it rained for five days. He was 97. He said he was 106, but he was an old person and can exaggerate all he wants! That's part of the beauty. Who cares? And he died, just when he said he would.

"We all feed the spirits. Your lease agreement on this earth is your death. You agree to die. Nobody is going to escape. The Mayan have no verb 'to be,' so we don't have any 'to be or not to be' questions, because 'to be or not to be' is out of the question! So half of what the modern world spends its time philosophizing about is completely irrelevant to the Maya. Since there is no 'to be' there is no 'not to be.' Ceasing doesn't come into it. The word 'death' in Mayan is the same word as 'now'—so nowness is death. Worrying about death only applies to people that have not got home yet."

"Take no food and no water, and stay out in the bush from sundown to sundown. Try to remember everything that happens around you. But don't have a single thought about yourself. Put a circle around yourself and promise not to look outside that circle. You'll be surprised what stuff goes on. There's a lot of life. The awareness of who you are. Where you actually are. Of everything being interconnected. Your body being the earth and your soul the wind blowing through it."

ERNESTO ALVARADO
APACHE TRADITION

Ernesto Alvarado is a qualified Doctor of Psychology working with people suffering mental health problems. He is also a Cali: a shaman and spiritual healer in his native Gavilian Mexican-Apache tradition. From as early as six years old Ernesto was fascinated by the work of the native healers. In 1975 he became apprentice to a shaman, until eventually his own spirit guide took over. This was a dramatic transformation, which made him question his own sanity. Having been trained in western psychology he put himself through every conceivable rational test, but his shamanic experiences were just not explainable in these terms.

Ernesto doesn't claim to have any answers, only that if we are willing to learn from nature we can begin to awaken spiritually and allow the spirits to guide our lives as they do his. Although play-ful and irreverent, he is also a man of deep compassion and down-to-earth integrity. He has no time for money-making charlatans, whether in his own Native American tradition or in others. As he warns: "If there's money involved—it's probably not spiritual!" He teaches that we are all members of one human family and should help each other from a natural sense of kinship, not the desire for personal gain. For Ernesto, a true shaman is not someone who exhibits magical powers and can control the spirits, but someone who has simply learned to give freely of themselves.

In Ernesto's view, Shamanism is the ancient tradition of healing practiced within the family or tribe. It is the kindness that occurs naturally within a genuine community in which everyone is seen as family. It is this spontaneous generosity of spirit which marks a true healer.

I know I don't know,
and he don't know,
and you don't know.

Why, why, why oh why?
Why do we live?
Why do we die?

I know I don't know,
and he don't know,
and you don't know.

NEW WORDS TO
TRADITIONAL CHANT
GIVEN TO ERNESTO
BY THE SPIRITS

LISTENING TO WISDOMKEEPER ERNESTO ALVARADO

"For myself, the role of the shaman is to take people to a door and encourage them, and show them options. Of course, I do practice a lot of things that give the trappings of a shaman. I do vision quests or help people with them. I do sweat lodges or help people with them. But I'm not the core. The people are. I'm a teacher. It's an assister role. It's not a dominator. It's not to hold the

> "I'm not in control. I'd hate to control the spirits. I don't have the power to control. I'm the one who's being controlled. I'm the one who's being led."

answer. The answer is in the individual. We can facilitate that for each other and hold hands.

"Some people think a shaman is a person that only journeys in between the worlds. Well fine. But I think a shaman is that 'Aunt Sarah' who brings you your tea and gives you a kiss and a pat on the head. All families were originally given someone with some knowledge of herbs, or teas, or massage, or comforting, caring with a touch or words. Healing was always on the basis that you heal the family because you are family. Because of the bloodline, not because of money.

"Of course the extended family is the tribe. People sometimes don't fathom that a tribe is just an extension of a lot of uncles and aunts. They have a feeling that it might be like a city—all types of cultures and people in this huge thing called a tribe. But no. A tribe is just another word for extended family. So the philosophy was one of communal group sharing and helping each other.

Barrel cacti and the giant cactus saguaro, at Tempe, Arizona.

"I think part of what we're rediscovering is to get people to take care of their families again. To get people to heal each other in their own way; not defined by someone else. Not in a controlling fashion. It could be a hug. It could be a kiss. It could be money—I've given people money. It's how you would treat your closest friend, your closest love. That's how healers should work."

Ernesto believes very strongly that when the shaman begins to sell his or her healing abilities the true relationship of being kindred is destroyed. Linking healing to a money transaction corrupts the natural impulse to help and creates unnatural divisions between the helper and the helped, which do not occur in a traditional tribal setting.

"There are many people who abuse Shamanism. They're into making a profit. Another way to make a dollar. There are a lot of people who are into power and control. They have lost the essence of healing. You should only do things because you feel you should do it. The money gets in the way and the training becomes catered to making money. You keep a distance. Why do you keep a distance? Because you can kick someone out the door if they don't pay you. And if they can't pay, then you're not going to see them. It's all playing into making money and it has less and less to do with helping people.

"I don't charge anything. So, if you know somebody and they call me tomorrow, I'll make an appointment. I'll give them the earth. I'll give them whatever they need to heal themselves. See they are treated like family. And when you treat someone like a family you change the professional boundaries. I've stayed with a family for three days just helping them heal themselves. Ask your local psychologist to do that! Ask him to see you after 5 o'clock on Friday! 'Sorry I don't have time for you.' They're afraid to get close.

"I don't think a healer is someone trying to figure out a way to make money. It's rich insideness that is of the Spirit. So leave it that way. And honor it. And let it guide you. Don't take it and try to make a profit. Ceremonies change where people are selling them. That's a fact. There is one group in America that advertise: 'Sweat $350. Super sweat $550'! I'm serious! Do I get a written guarantee that the Spirit will be there?"

Ernesto warns that there is a lot of hocus-pocus surrounding Shamanism. As a qualified psychologist he is aware just how easily people are led by suggestion into shallow, inauthentic shamanic experiences. What a genuine shaman does is usually very practical and down to earth. Extraordinary things do occur but not because of the shaman's magical powers. It is simply that life is magical and if the shaman tunes in to the spirits magical things naturally happen around him.

"We're looking for something that's real and spiritual, but there are plenty of people who

"We've got to learn from the spirits how to live in peace with each other. When we do, we become a family of sharing."

are ready to lead you on. It's a fundamental trick. The most popular is group suggestion. Like, you're doing a sweat lodge and someone claims to see something - 'Oh, did you see that bear there?' Now you're on the spot. There you are. Ten to fifteen people there in darkness. And the suggestion is you should have seen that spirit-bear. And you say: 'Well, I saw something.' So the next person takes the lead from that person and goes: 'Yeah I think I saw something too'. The next person then says:

'Yeah, I saw a bear.' And people walk away saying: 'We saw a bear'. They don't say: 'I saw a bear,' because they didn't see a bear. But the shaman manipulated the group. It's easy to do.

"Group psychology—that's how people are controlled. People get carried away doing things that are phoney baloney. When I demonstrate how it's done, people are so shocked—'Oh, I thought you really had these powers.' Take the power to look at someone and to say: 'Ah, in the next year you're going to feel pretty ill.' God, who doesn't! What's the possibility? 90%? 'You have a problem with a relationship.' Who doesn't? Saying these things empowers the individual who wants to be seen as a shaman, but it's just the law of probability. Native American medicine men can be very, very controlling. But in my tribe our medicine men would never allow that. It would be really bad for the tribe. It just leads to confusion.

"You want magic? Then go find a charlatan! If you want to carry all those beliefs, fine. But is it going to get you through? I don't know. People get carried away by what they attribute to you. I'll go out and do a real simple counseling thing, but before you know it people are saying all these phenomenal things that I did. Whereas in fact it was just very practical. I guess it's the need to have extreme belief in others when you don't have it in yourself.

Pre-Colombian Native rock art, or petroglyphs, in the petrified forest of Arizona.

"Things happen. Mysterious things. It's wonderful when things happen, but it's not in my control. It's in the spirits' control. It's the path I'm on and I really think it goes back to being a family healer. I try to be myself and encourage people to be themselves. Let's just be kind to each other, encourage each other, and try to be family. I think that the spirits and ancestors are trying to get us back to real basics.

"I believe that the Great Spirit left us with three basic commitments. One was to take care of Motherearth–Fatherearth. Secondly, to take care of our bodies. Your body is the shell of the spirit and the spirit is not going to be healthy if your body is not healthy. Very basic. The third—and

people often count this as the most difficult—is don't score off other people. They are a being, so don't try to manipulate them. Don't try to control them. They are not yours. Leave them alone."

Ernesto leads those he works with in Native American shamanic practices such as the sweat lodge and the vision quest. The sweat lodge is a ceremony in which participants purify themselves, body and soul, through sweating within a small dark lodge especially constructed for the purpose. The vision quest is a traditional initiation undertaken by young boys and girls in order to enter adulthood. It involves spending a night, or a number of nights, alone in the wilderness

"When we die we're going to change. The energy's going to change. But it's going to go on, 'cos it's the Life Force. We came from there. We feel that in ourselves. That energy is going to go on. It's in the shell. The shell is not me. The shell doesn't define me. It just holds me together for now."

without food and water. This is an intense spiritual practice also performed by many adults who are in search of insight and visions.

"The sweat lodge is like going back to the womb. There's a communal group supporting you and you're asking the spirits to help you heal. And part of it we usually do are 'thank yous.' It's one way of blessing each other and asking for guidance. Personally, for me it's a place where people come for healing. For some tribes the sweat lodge is only a purification that leads you to a vision quest or something like that. For some it's a phase, for others it's the whole thing.

"The vision quest is an initial initiation. I've done many, many vision quests for others. Today people lose their sense of adulthood because there is no initiation. There is no passage. We try to start with thirteen-year-olds. Some will survive the night

The saguaro organ-pipe cactus and the ocotillo, a cactus like tree, against the evening sky in Tucson, Arizona.

and some won't. And then we've had fifty- and sixty-year-olds doing their first vision quest. You come face to face with fear. It's in the middle of the night and you are out in the wilderness with bears and cougars around. You feel: 'My God, am I going to survive the night?' So you kinda reflect and think about what it takes to survive the bear. And hopefully what happens is you have to face the bear. You have to face your fears. Things that have been put in your dark attic appear in your mind's eye.

"People say the most wonderful thing you get there is a vision of what you're going to do when you grow up. Well OK—sometimes. You might get a spirit guide come and help you. But most of the time you've gotta face the bear. It's mighty dark and the bear is out there. And you think if the bear wants me I'll run. But the bear can run. Or I'll climb a tree. Well, a bear can climb a tree all right. If the bear wants me he's going to get me, so I'd better get on with life and be comfortable with myself.

"I was willing to go wherever the spirits sent me. I no longer asked, I just did it. It became a primary force for me. It became a movement inside me."

"That's what happens in a true vision quest. You learn where those fears come from and what you can and can't control. I'm not going to worry about the bear. I'm going to move on with life. So you move on with life and you begin to respect nature when it comes. It's very scary and many don't make it. The first time they go up on a vision quest they come down after a few hours, afraid of the dark and the night and the bear. Then another night they try it again and then they are ready to be comforted."

An important formative experience for Ernesto on his shamanic journey was participating in a major peyote ceremony of the Native American church. Peyote, a powerful natural psychedelic, has been ingested by shamans for centuries to bring visions and help them connect with the spirits. Besides introducing him to the profound peyote experience, this ceremony was also an opportunity for Ernesto to meet many renowned medicine men from different tribes.

"Peyote is a medicine I have used which played an important role in my life. On the reservation it is successfully used to cure alcoholism. Peyote stimulates visions. There are so many dimensions to everything and it sharpens you so you can read the messages right. I have met with professors who have written quite a bit on it. But because of their profession they don't want to be too descriptive, because people will call them real whacko. They say they are a professional observer. Well, I'm a professional too. I've still kept a professional business. Hey! Come on! Be honest! It seemed like the spirits were there.

"For me it was kinda like a dramatic turn on a road that was happening gradually. I went to a major ceremony. I didn't know it was a peyote ritual. I just knew that I was supposed to go to this certain place. My spirit said: 'Go here and accept what's going to happen.' And I was naive or trusting enough, whatever way you want to perceive it, to do that. And the connections were miraculous.

"I had to travel a thousand miles to the area. Leaving everything to go to a major city. I was a stranger in this city and I met somebody who said: 'What are you doing here?' Well, he was kinda Indian-looking so I thought, 'Well, take a chance.' So I said: 'I'm here because the spirits sent me and I'm not sure beyond there.' And this individual said: 'Well, do you know there's going to be a ceremony within a week or two? But you've got to go over to a

The characteristically stiff, sword-shaped leaves of the yucca, New Mexico.

reservation two or three hundred miles away. I can't guide you there but I can get permission and introductions for you to go there. But if you don't go this might well be the last ceremony in this state.'

"Well, I sorta scared everybody 'cos I found my way through the mountains. It was difficult 'cos it was in the middle of the night in a pine covered area. So I just tried to feel the energy and it was OK. I knew that I was going to the ceremony. I had no awareness of what I was supposed to do. I introduced myself as a medicine man in training. I said I'd been sent by the spirits. I'd just got onto the path.

"My experience of peyote convinced me that it was something natural. A powerful herb. And it did begin to make me look at things from a different perspective. Mainly I understood you've got to love people. The first words that came into my head were 'love' and 'divine light.' After peyote, love took on an entirely different dimension. It was just a natural thing. This peacefulness inside with this feeling that was love. And yet that gets so trivial—using that word 'love.' It really isn't that at all. It's naturally being a part of everything."

"We sweat. We do vision quests. We call the spirits. We dance in the wind. We have fun."

Ernesto does not see himself as teaching answers, but rather as pointing to the perpetual mystery. He compares our dilemma to having been given an intriguing black box, the contents of which we will never discover.

A flowering yucca, known as the "century plant," in Arizona.

"Spirit gives you a black box. There's something in there, but you're never going to know what it is. Some people shake that box to try and guess—'Oh yeah, in there is a spirit that looks like me.' They'll live their life that way. But we don't know what's in the black box. That's the thing we are never going to know. People profess they know. Some people are redefining it all the time. Every other day they shake that box and say: 'I thought I knew.' Others will learn just to leave it alone and accept it. 'Cos we aren't going to know until finally we are in that space with that black box.

"You know, Great Spirit has a great sense of humor. He sets us up with this profound mystery. Then he creates us to shit and pee and have all these needs. For me, I can accept that when my energy leaves this shell there's some probability that I shall be given some answers. So let's try to be comfortable and leave the black box alone. There's a song the spirits gave me which goes like: 'I know I don't know, and he don't know, and you don't know.' You see the Pope don't know. Jesus don't know. He don't know. I know he don't know. I know the apostles don't know. I know our medicine men don't know. Why? I don't know!!!"

PRACTICAL SHAMANISM
BEING WHERE THE SPIRITS WANT YOU

"Ask yourself once a month: 'Am I where I'm supposed to be? Am I doing what I'm supposed to be doing?' If you can answer 'Yes' then you are on your way. But if you answer 'No' to either one, either you have to go where things are going to happen for you, or start doing what you should be doing. And that's a start. And then begin to look for things that are beyond coincidence. I would say it should happen three times. Then you think: 'Maybe I'd better listen because those spirit guys are trying to contact me.'"

LORRAINE MAFI-WILLIAMS
AUSTRALIAN ABORIGINAL TRADITION

Lorraine Mafi-Williams is a senior Aboriginal elder, shaman, teacher, healer and keeper of the ancient creation stories. Lorraine's father is from the Bunjalung clan who come from the north coast of New South Wales, her mother is a Thungutti from the south, and she is married to a Githrabaul man from farther west. She holds the story lineage of the Knarkbaul, whose name derives from the scream of an eagle—'narkkkk!' She is also the guardian of the story of Mount Warning, a majestic peak shaped like an eagle's head whose Aboriginal name means simply 'Eagle.' Along with her spiritual work, Lorraine is also very active in politics as a spokesperson for her people in the battle for Aboriginal land rights. As she puts it: "I'm a senior elder and teacher but I'm also radical! It all comes together —arts and politics, as well as Shamanism."

Despite brutal oppression by the European invaders, the Aboriginal Australians have maintained their ancestral wisdom. This has not been easy because their spirituality is firmly rooted in the land and many of their sacred places have now been desecrated and destroyed. However, Lorraine explains that their ancient teachings are still being passed from elder to elder.

The Aboriginal peoples of Australia call their elders "uncles" and "aunties." The title "Auntie Lorraine" has a gentle familiarity about it which suits her open, approachable manner. As she talks about her ancestral wisdom Lorraine's voice sparkles with life and warmth. Her Shamanism requires us to understand our common humanity and overcome our differences. Only this can help us through the cataclysmic "Earth changes," which the Aboriginal elders believe are already upon us.

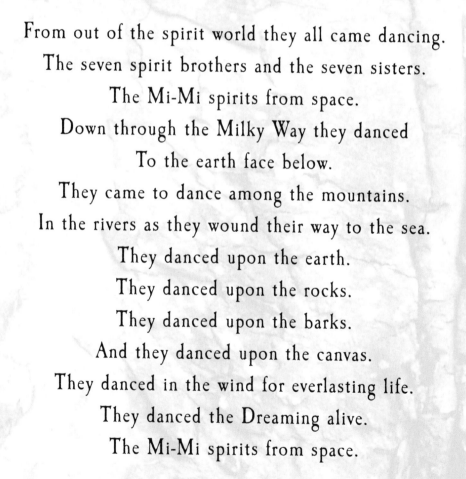

From out of the spirit world they all came dancing.

The seven spirit brothers and the seven sisters.

The Mi-Mi spirits from space.

Down through the Milky Way they danced

To the earth face below.

They came to dance among the mountains.

In the rivers as they wound their way to the sea.

They danced upon the earth.

They danced upon the rocks.

They danced upon the barks.

And they danced upon the canvas.

They danced in the wind for everlasting life.

They danced the Dreaming alive.

The Mi-Mi spirits from space.

Lorraine Mafi-Williams

LISTENING TO WISDOMKEEPER LORRAINE MAFI-WILLIAMS

Ceremonial body paint being worn by an Aborigine at a dance festival.

"Us Australian Aboriginal people, we live in the spirit world more than we do in the living. We depend more on the spirits to guide us than anything outside."

"In our tradition a shaman person means a teacher, a healer, a wisdomkeeper of the knowledge of our culture and our spiritualism. We've never ever had a religious leader like Jesus, Buddha, Muhammad—like that. We've never ever had such a leader. Nor on the political scene. Neither king or queen or president or anything like that either. We just relied upon the wisdom and knowledge of the elders. We just depended on the old people to keep our tradition intact. And our tradition is still very much intact, in so much as in our own community the deeper culture is still taught.

"The traditional role of the shaman has not changed for my people. But we can't go into the country to the sacred sites where the magic was given to us, because a lot of the places where we received these teachings are now settled on. There are towns and villages on these places. So we have what I call contemporary cultural shamanic teachings to fit in with modern time.

Rock engravings showing hunting scenes at Mootwingee National Park, New South Wales.

But it's still based on a very old ancient tradition that has been passed down to us.

"The land is very important spiritually to Aboriginal peoples. I was lucky to be taught on the remainder of land still available for us to be taught on. But now these places of magic, as we call them, no longer exist. So when I teach, I teach with the land that's available to me—parks, nature reserves, a forest, or something like that."

Like all Aboriginal children brought up in a traditional environment, Lorraine was introduced to the indigenous wisdom of her tribe at an early age. But

she did not want to be "chosen" by the spirits to become a shaman. In fact she regarded it as "a pain in the neck!" Her calling was eventually too strong to ignore, however, and she underwent the necessary training to become a healer and keeper of the ancestral stories.

"When we're little children, from the age of three years, we are taught the basics. About our lineage and songs and stories and things like that. So we are encouraged and brought up with it until we are in our teens. And then we settle down to what sort of career we're going to have. Not all of us go along the shamanic path. Not all of us are chosen. I was first taught traditional medicine as a child but I didn't really want to go on a healing path.

An X-ray Aboriginal painting of a spirit figure at Ubirr Rock, Kakadu National Park.

"I was in my early twenties when I was asked by various elders of our people to carry on the knowledge. I was happily going along my own way. I was aiming to have a flower nursery. That was my great ambition. I wanted to have that until my early twenties and then the spirits were calling. So then I became a writer of children's stories. And that led to filmmaking. And I was a producer and director working for ABC—the Australian Broadcasting Commission. And I was quite happy with that. But the spirits kept calling. And for two years I just said: 'No. I really don't want to go on a shamanic path.' But the elders were watching me and they were sorta throwing out hints. 'Well, you better pull your finger out and start it because you're chosen no matter which way you look at it.'

"Eventually I accepted it and I just said to the guides: 'OK, I'll work for you.' And they said: 'No. You don't work for us. We work for you.' So I thought: 'Well, that's OK. It's pretty good being a boss.' And I gave two conditions. I said: 'Fasting's out because I like my food. And climbing mountains is out. I can't climb mountains because I'm lazy.' So that was OK. But I eventually ended up doing both!

"It took me about a period of three years to learn everything. I was asked to do traditional healing first. I heal with fire. I have been taught fire medicine and how to use fire for all sorts of things. And when you get taught traditional healing in our system you have to learn everything that relates to the Earth changes and the environment and the elements and humanity. Everything. So I've gone through all those stages of teachings. I am now at a very high level and I suppose I am, to use a western term, a 'high' shaman. And I'm still

"The spirit guides are our ancestors' spirits."

going. I'm fifty-eight years old and I've reached the top now, so I'm retiring. Sort of!"

Lorraine teaches that we are each a spirit which is resident in a human body and that we reincarnate over and over again. Unlike some other traditions, however, the Aboriginal Australians believe that they always reincarnate within the same family or clan. Each clan has various animal totems which link it to the spirits.

"We come from the spirit world as spirit first and then manifest into a human body. A material body. We believe strongly in reincarna-tion, but within our own lineage. Like—on the woman's side I might be the reincarnation of my seventh grandmother. My great, great, great, great, great grandmother—going back seven times.

Rain forest in Barrington Tops National Park, New South Wales.

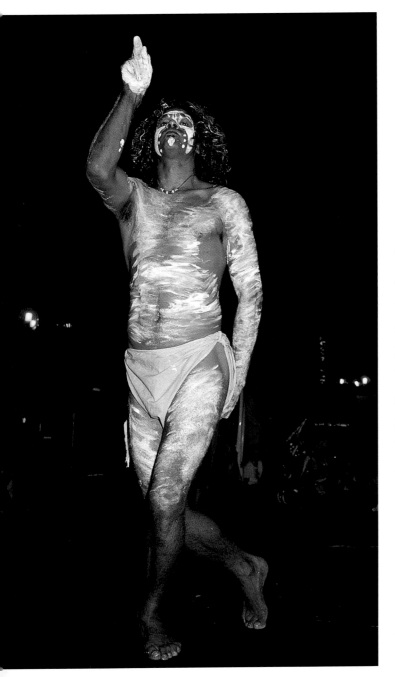

An Aborigine wearing traditional body paint performs a dance.

"Take a country that has been at war. When there's a lot of human blood spilled into the earth, the earth can't cope with this type of energy. So there is generally an earthquake in that country."

That's how we believe. That we only reincarnate in our own family lineage. In western society a lot of white people come and say: 'I was an Aboriginal in my last life' or 'I was a Chinese or an Indian in my last life.' Indian is very popular. Everybody was a North American Indian in their last life! And I say: 'No. But you are fortunate because you have a Indian spirit guide. A spirit which looks after you.' We have spirits like that. What we call our ancestor spirits. You see, our grandparents, our uncles and aunties that have gone—their spirits are around us all the time and we get guidance from them. They talk to us and tell us what to do and look after us. But this is not in the western world as far as I know. They've gotten away from it.

"We also have animal spirits or fish spirits. We have what we call totems. They're like family crests. Every family has a bird, a fish, and an animal for their totem. Our ancestors' spirits come to us through these three totems. For example, my father's totem is a little black rock wallaby—like a little kangaroo. So if I see that little black wallaby I know that's my father come to look after me, or be with me, or protect me, or something. The spirit of my father is in that wallaby, or in a bird, or in a fish. That's what we believe. You see our spirits are never far from us. Never away from us. Never leave us. They are there. That's not in the western world and I think that's very sad."

Aboriginal wisdom reaches right back to the very beginning, known as the "Dreamtime." Lorraine teaches that the Aboriginal peoples originally came from the stars as the "Mi-Mi spirits from space." Their specific task is to maintain the "energy grid," which lies within the Earth's crust. This is especially important at this time because we are currently undergoing momentous "Earth changes," which will significantly affect both the planet and humanity.

"The Dreamtime is like the beginning. Now our old people, when they talk, they go right back to very ancient times. And they talk about when the world was one. Before the cataclysm that split the earth into the continents we have now. The big flood time. And they talk about when all of the four nations were living close together on Earth. Until the split came and we were all divided.

"Our older people have kept the very, very ancient belief that we came from the heavens.

The characteristic red surface and scrub vegetation of the desert of Western Australia.

From the stars. Yeah. Our heavenly existence as we call it. There were the four races here on Earth already. There was animals here on Earth. Just like in the Bible, God created the heavens, the Earth, the beasts of the field, and then man. And as we understand it there was the black race first, the red race, the yellow race, and then the white race. The four races were here on Earth. Us Aboriginal people, we are like a fifth race. We came in between the black and the red race. So we're the fifth race sorta thing. We came direct from the heavens. We are not a sub-branch of any other black race in the world. We're totally unique.

"Our specific job on Earth was to maintain the energy grid that keeps the earth in balance. The energy grid consists of all the minerals, the jewels, the crystals, and so on, that make up the Earth's crust. We simply call it 'Baime the

Rainbow Serpent.' The snake symbolizes the energy grid which snakes around underneath the earth. You find this in other cultures. Like in Asian culture they have the dragon.

"Our people simply walked along the Earth and they could find if there was fault in the energy gird. And they were able to energize the grid with crystals, or just with human body energy going into the ground. Because we kept that knowledge we understand that the earth is undergoing changes now. And those changes are related to the creation of a new world. We are coming into a different time, but with the same Earth.

"But while these Earth upheavals are going on it's also going on in the heavens as well. You see it's all changing at once. The heavens started their shift with the planetary line-up and the comets that have been seen not long ago. That's all happening and happened. And humanity is going through changes as well. And it's not very good changes. But it's a purifying change. The wars that are going on now, and all the sicknesses and diseases, as well as the earthquakes, floods, storms, and things like that. These are all the changes that we need to understand and be helped through.

Azure seas at Smoky Cape, in the Hat Head National Park, New South Wales.

"We believe that the Earth undergoes a seven-thousand-year shift toward a new rejuvenated world. A new Earth. The Australian Aboriginals' job is to maintain the energy grid so that as the Earth shifts it can move in its natural way. These changes are happening now. We've had two shifts and we've got one major shift to come. And that will put the Earth back in balance so that it rotates in its proper way. This will have an effect on human consciousness. Humanity's consciousness is now in disarray, if I can put it like that. Humanity is all out of balance. But that will be rectified soon. I don't know how long. It will all come back into balance and reach fruition.

"You see, when we learn to become a shaman we have to learn all this, so that we can help the Earth through its changes and help humanity through its changes. But we can't do anything about the universe changes. The universe can take care of itself! But here on earth it is our elders and shaman people who bring everybody through."

The Aboriginal elders regard it as their role to help the white race understand the changes that are upon us and to begin to care for the Earth and all of humanity. At this time of chaos they teach that God is not a big man or woman in the sky, but a Being of love who wishes us to come together with respect for each other and the world we all share.

Rainford's butterfly fish, photographed on the Great Barrier Reef, off Queensland.

"The maintenance of the Earth is crucial to humanity. Rather than fighting with each other, we should be concentrating on the Earth. Looking after the Earth. Because we all live on it. That's where we all get our sustenance. Our home. Our food. Our everything comes from the Earth. And if the Earth goes we go! It's as simple as that.

"It was about a hundred years ago that the elders said we have to help white Australians through these changes and shifts as well. The elders want it to be that when the time comes no white person has the excuse to say that they haven't been told by the Aboriginal people. If they mess the world up, we try and make them fix it up. That's how our people see it. We've got to teach them. Share our culture. Put it out. So we've been sort of working together. But segregated, because there is still a lot of racism around. But we are breaking down barriers and we will come together as one people.

"I go into schools and teach a contemporary approach to ancient Aboriginal wisdom that links us in with white Australians. We try and be open to teaching anyone that wants to learn from the Aboriginal culture. And we have to put it in a contemporary way."

"When humanity is in chaos like it is now, the simplest teaching given by the Aboriginals is to respect each other. Nobody is better than anybody else. Love one another. Especially in these times of chaos. And I don't just mean the love between husband and wife. I mean the humanity love as well. And just the caring toward each other. So there is no war going on. No discrimination. No racism. Everybody is equal. And that's what God wants us to do.

"You see, we believe there is a God in heaven, just like everybody else. But we believe that God is the pure golden illuminating light of love. It's a Being. God's not a man or a woman. It's a beautiful Being of love. And all humanity should know that and love each other. That's the ultimate aim of the above and the below. That's the ultimate aim of humanity."

A mother and joey of the eastern gray kangaroo species, in New South Wales.

"Simply take your shoes off and stand on the earth. Bare earth if you can find it. It doesn't matter if you can't. And you will feel the energy coming up through your body. Or just sit on the earth. Or if possible lie on it with your spine bare on the ground. And you will feel the energy from the Rainbow Serpent. The energy grid. You will feel it come up into your body to lift you. And that's how our people remain in contact with the Earth."

ADDRESSES

Contacts for further information concerning the contributors to this book:

Jamie Sams Cherokee: *Choctaw and Seneca Traditions*
Website: http://www.jamiesams.com/nat

Malidoma Patrice Somé: *West African Dagara Tradition*
11881 Skyline Suite A
Oakland, CA 94619
U.S.A.

Miguel A. Kavlin: *Amazonian Tradition*
P.O. Box 5521
La Paz
Bolivia
In Canada tel: (416) 928 5927
In Bolivia tel: 591-2-792164 (leave message)
In Bolivia fax: 591-2-772091
E-mail: sacharun@total.net
Website: http://www.sacharuna.com

Haleakala Hew Len Ph.D.: *Hawaiian Tradition*
The Foundation of I Inc.
(Freedom of the Cosmos)
Home base Hawaii
P.O. Box 10861
Honolulu, HI 89616-0861
U.S.A.
Tel/fax: (808) 395 9278

U.S., Central, and South America
P.O. Box 30337
Philadelphia, PA 19103-1419
U.S.A.
Tel/fax: (215) 731 3202
Website: http://www.hooponopono.org

Lama Khemsar Rinpoche: *Tibetan Bon Tradition*
Yungdrung Bon Study Centre Scotland
c/o Flat G2
216 Berkeley Street
Glasgow, G3 7HQ
U.K.
Tel: 0141 226 5719

Yungdrung Bon Study Centre England
c/o Building 16 The Lincolnsfield Centre
Bushey Hall Drive
Bushey
Herts. WD2 2ER
U.K.
Tel: 01923 228858
Fax: 01923 467965

Andy Baggott: *Celtic Tradition*
PO Box 2453
Frome
Somerset, BA11 3YN
U.K.
E-mail: brightowl@celtlodg.globalnet.co.uk

Aiko Aiyana: *Santo Daime Tradition*
Santo Daime
Ceu da Santa Maria
Van Kinsbergenstraat 16–11
1057 PP Amsterdam
The Netherlands
Tel/fax: 3120 616 1413
E-mail: cdsmaria@cetron.nl
UK E-mail: essence@dircon

Martín Prechtel: *Tzutujil Mayan Tradition*
contact via his publishers:
U.K.: c/o Element Books
Tel: 01747 851339
U.S.A.: c/o Tarcher/Putnam
Tel: 212 366 2539

Ernesto Alvarado: *Apache Tradition*
1453 East 130th Dr.
Thornton, CO 80241-1109
U.S.A.
Tel: (303) 451 9030
E-mail: neto3@aol.com

ADDRESSES

Lorraine Mafi-Williams: *Australian Aboriginal Tradition*
Nunarng Cultural Sanctuary
PO Box 42
Suffolk Park
New South Wales 2481
Australia

INFORMATION ON MODERN SHAMANISM

Sacred Hoop Magazine
PO Box 16
Narberth
Pembrokeshire
SA67 8YG
England
Tel/fax: 01834 860320

Shaman's Drum Magazine
PO Box 1939
Mill Valley
CA 94942
USA
Tel: (415) 380 828
Website: http://www.Shamanism.org

PICTURE CREDITS

The publishers are grateful to the following for permission to reproduce copyright material:

Bruce Coleman: pp 14 (Guido Cazi),
15 (John Cancalosi), 20 (John Cancalosi),
51, 57, 59, 61 (Steve Alden), 66 (Anders Blomquist),
70 (Anders Blomquist), 71 (Hans Reinhard),
87 (Christer Frederiksson), 114 (N. McAllister),
116 (Rod Williams), 127 (Jules Cowan),
128 (Jules Cowan), 129 (Jules Cowan),
134 (George Bingham), 136 (Kevin Burchett),
139 (Quentin M. Bennett), 140 ((John Cancalosi)

Image Bank: pp 16 (Pete Turner), 46 (Marc Solomon),
84, 91 (C. van der Lende), 141 (Thomas Schmitt)

Images: pp 7, 12, 54, 62, 73, 74, 75

NHPA: pp 48 (Martin Wendler),
60 (James Carmichael), 86 (N.A. Callow),
88 (Stephen Dalton), 89 (David Woodfall),
97 (Stepehn Dalton), 123 (Stephen Krasemann),
132 (Klaus Unlenhut), 133 (Otto Rogge)

Oxford Scientific Films: pp 103 (John Chellmanm),
137 (R.J.B. Goodale)

Robert Harding: pp 19, 21, 32, 45, 50, 69, 76, 79, 94,
98, 106, 107, 115, 120, 124

South American Pictures: pp 13t (Tony Morrison),
13 (Tony Morrison), 23 (Robert Francis),
41 (Tony Morrison), 42 (Tony Morrison),
43 (Tony Morrison), 49 (Tony Morrison),
96 (Index Editora), 100 (Bill Leimbach),
108 (Robert Francis)

Trip: pp 2 (W. Jacobs), 18 (J. Denis), 26 (M. Jelliffe),
27 (B. Seed), 29 (W. Jacobs), 31 (B. Vikander),
33 (B. Seed), 34 (B. Seed), 36 (B. Seed),
37 (B. Vikander), 40 (W. Jacobs), 44 (C. Rennie),
47 (J. Drew), 55 (E. Young), 56 (J. Greenberg),
58 (Alistair Cook), 63 (A. Bloomfield),
67 (B. Vikander), 68 (B. Vikander), 77 (B. Vikander),
78 (B. Vikander), 85 (J.C. Wood), 95 (Ask Images),
99 (Ask Images), 101 (Ask Images), 102 (Ask Images),
109 (W. Jacobs), 110 (Ask Images), 111 (S. Passmore),
113 (W. Jacobs), 121 (T. Mackie), 138 (Eric Smith)

INDEX

Africa 24-37
Animals 16-17, 20, 22, 83-4
Ayahuasca 13, 38-51, 92, 94, 103

Blinking 14, 15, 22
Buddhism 68-70

Death 49, 115, 116
Diet 86-9
Drums 17, 83, 96

Earth changes 137, 138-9
Emotion 27-8, 44, 47, 60
Energy grid 137-9, 141
Enlightenment trap 20

Immune system 87-8
Indigo Bowl 63

Kahunas 52, 54-5, 62
Kontombili 28-37

Lamas 64-6, 77

Medicine Cards 10, 16

Nagas 71-2, 75, 76-8
Nutrition 86-8

Offerings 48-9, 107, 112, 115-16

Perception 12-13, 22, 28, 52, 54-5, 60
Peyote 126-7
Pleiades 45
Power plants 42, 44, 92
Prayer 48-9, 51, 78, 102, 108

Rainbow Serpent 138, 141
Responsibility 59-62, 85, 97

Senses 15, 31, 85
Shape-shifting 13
Sugar 87-8
Sweat lodges 123-5

Thought 52-5, 57-60, 72
Tibet 64, 66-9, 72, 75, 78
Totems 136-7
Trail of Tears 10

Vision Quests 123-5-6

Wishing Ceremony 90